BRAIN QUEST

GRADE 1
WORKBOOK

Written by Lisa Trumbauer
Consulting Editor: Betsy Rogers

Workman Publishing • New York

This book belongs to:

First Name

Last Name

ISBN 978-1-5235-1735-0

New and updated text by Jen Agresta and Jennifer Szymanski; educational review by Anne Haywood, Rebecca Keller, and Peg Keiner

Illustrations by Stephen Lewis, Kimble Mead, and Scott Dubar, with cover illustrations by Edison Yan

Workbook series design by Raquel Jaramillo

30th Anniversary Edition Revision produced for Workman by WonderLab Group, LLC, and Fan Works Design, LLC.

Workman books are available at special discounts when purchased in bulk for premiums and sales promotions as well as for fundraising or educational use. Special editions or book excerpts can also be created to specification. For details, please contact special.markets@hbgusa.com.

WORKMAN, BRAIN QUEST, and IT'S FUN TO BE SMART! are registered trademarks of Workman Publishing Co., Inc., a subsidiary of Hachette Book Group, Inc.

Distributed in Europe by Hachette Livre, 58 rue Jean Bleuzen, 92 178 Vanves Cedex, France.

Distributed in the United Kingdom by Hachette Book Group, UK, Carmelite House, 50 Victoria Embankment, London EC4Y 0DZ.

Workman Publishing Co., Inc.
1290 Avenue of the Americas
New York, NY 10104
workman.com • brainquest.com

Printed in China on responsibly sourced paper.

First printing April 2023
10 9 8 7 6 5 4 3 2 1

Dear Parents and Caregivers,

Learning is an adventure—a quest for knowledge. At Brain Quest, we strive to guide children on that quest, to keep them motivated and curious, and to give them the confidence they need to do well in school and beyond. We're excited to partner with you and your child on this step of their lifelong knowledge quest.

BRAIN QUEST WORKBOOKS are designed to enrich children's understanding in all content areas by reinforcing the basics and previewing future learning. These are not textbooks, but rather true workbooks, and are best used to reinforce curricular concepts learned at school. Each workbook aligns with national and state learning standards and is written in consultation with an award-winning grade-level teacher.

In first grade, children become stronger decoders and learn to read and write more complex texts. They learn place value through 100 as they add, subtract, measure, count coins, and begin to tell time. They are curious about their community and the world around them—help them observe and talk about seasons, weather, plants, animals, and other areas of interest.

We're excited that BRAIN QUEST WORKBOOKS will play an integral role in your child's educational adventure. So, let the learning—and the fun—begin!

It's fun to be smart!®

—The editors of Brain Quest

HOW TO USE THIS BOOK

Welcome to the Brain Quest Grade 1 Workbook!

Encourage your child to complete the workbook at their own pace. Guide them to approach the work with a **growth mindset**, the idea that our abilities can change and grow with effort. Reinforce this by praising effort and problem-solving and explaining that mistakes are part of learning.

The **opening page** of each section has a note for parents and caregivers and another note just for kids.

Notes to parents highlight key skills and give suggestions for helping with each section.

Notes to children give learners a preview of each section.

Guide your child to place a sticker here to get excited about learning.

117

READING

What kinds of stories do you like to read? Are you ready to read stories about dragons, trees, robots, and more? Let's go!

PARENTS In this section, your child will improve their reading comprehension by practicing skills like sequencing, inferencing, and identifying text details. Have your child read the passages aloud and support them as needed.

For additional resources, visit www.BrainQuest.com/grade1

PLACE A STICKER HERE

Read the directions aloud if needed. Encourage your child to work as independently as possible.

Get your child talking! Ask about the images they see and connections between the workbook and their lives.

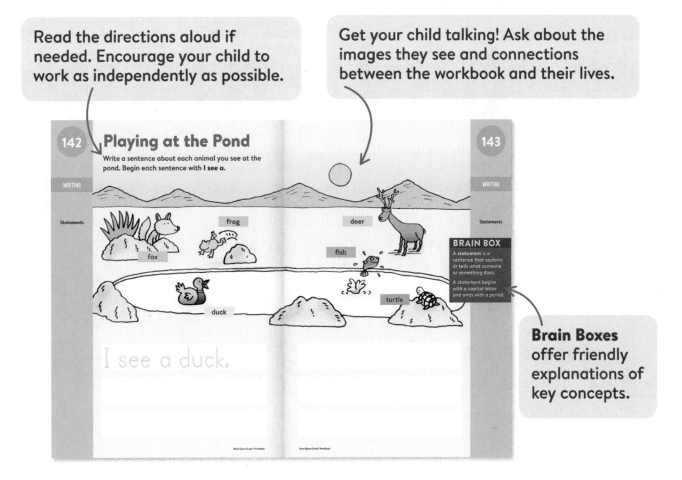

Brain Boxes offer friendly explanations of key concepts.

Cut out the Brain Quest **Mini-Deck** from the back to play and learn on the go!

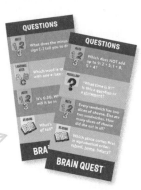

After each chapter, have your child place a sticker on the **progress map** to mark their achievement.

Encourage your child to use stickers to decorate the **certificate.** Hang it up when it's complete!

CONTENTS

PHONICS

What letter sounds do you know? Do you want to join me in some letter fun?

PARENTS Learning to identify letters and their sounds is important preparation for reading, and it is also FUN! Practice identifying letters on signs in the neighborhood or in your child's favorite books and games.

PLACE A STICKER HERE

For additional resources, visit www.BrainQuest.com/grade1

PHONICS

Beginning consonants

Super Safari!

The names of these animals all start with the **b**, **d**, or **f** sound.

Say the word for each animal.

What beginning sound do you hear?

Write the letter.

d og

eer

ox

BRAIN BOX

A **consonant** is any letter in the alphabet that is not a vowel.

at

ly

rog

ear

uck

eaver

To the Castle!

The things in this picture all start with the **h**, **j**, **k**, or **q** sound.

Say the word for each picture.

What beginning sound do you hear?

Write the letter.

Beginning consonants

arp

at

ar

itten

uilt

ueen

ing

ester

Monster Manor!

The things in this picture all start with the **l**, **m**, **n**, or **p** sound.

Say the word for each picture.

What beginning sound do you hear?

Write the letter.

Beginning
consonants

_____ onkey

_____ et

_____ uzzle

_____ onster

_____ izard

oon

ollipop

oodles

izza

Blast Off!

The things in this picture all start with the **r**, **s**, or **t** sound.

Say the word for each picture.

What beginning sound do you hear?

Write the letter.

Beginning consonants

eal

urtle

ocket

nake

accoon

iger

abbit

elescope

Wacky Wizard!

The things in this picture all start with the **v, w, x, y,** or **z** sound.

Say the word for each picture.

What beginning sound do you hear?

Write the letter.

ase

o–yo

histle

acuum

izard

ebra

ipper

arn

-ray

City and Country

Say the word for each picture.

If you hear a **hard c** sound, draw a line to the **country**.

If you hear a **soft c** sound, draw a line to the **city**.

country

city

BRAIN BOX

The letter **c** has two sounds: a **hard c** sound as in **country** and a **soft c** sound as in **city**.

Girl and Giant

Say the word for each picture.

If you hear a **hard g** sound, draw a line to the **girl**.

If you hear a **soft g** sound, draw a line to the **giant**.

girl

giant

BRAIN BOX

The letter g has two sounds: a **hard g** sound as in **girl** and a **soft g** sound as in **giant**.

Web and Kid

The words for these pictures all end in **b** or **d**.

Say the word for each picture.

What ending sound do you hear?

Write the letter.

Ending
consonants

bir

brea

cri

ki

cra

sle

we

bi

Fun in the Sun

The words for these pictures all end in **m** or **n**.

Say the word for each picture.

What ending sound do you hear?

Write the letter.

su ◯

pal

swi

fa

plu

cla

pe

22

PHONICS

Ending consonants

Ship and Boat

The words for these pictures all end in **p** or **t.**

Say the word for each picture.

What ending sound do you hear?

Write the letter.

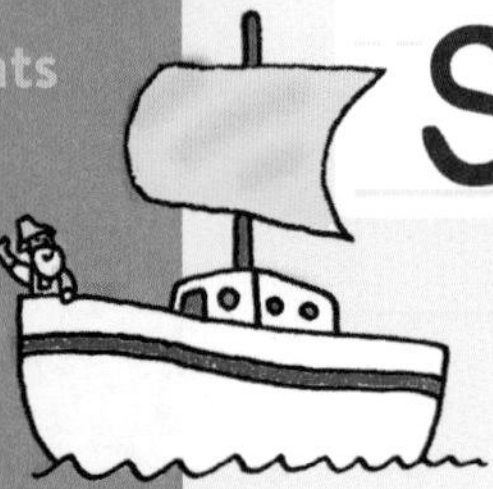
shi

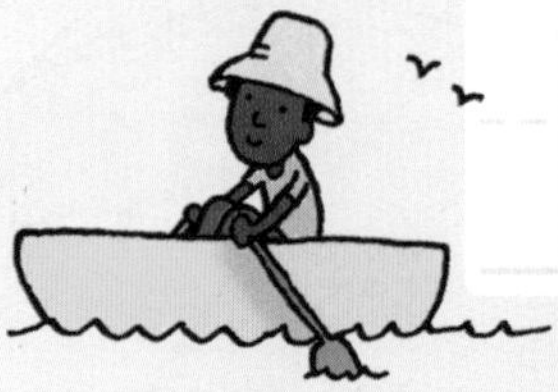
boa

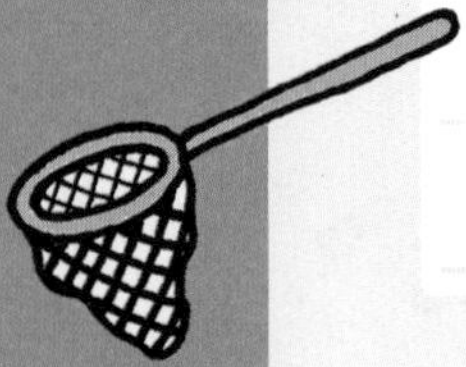
ne

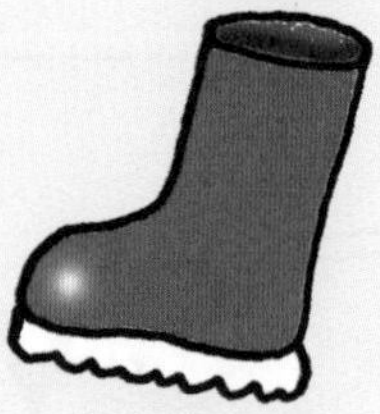
boo

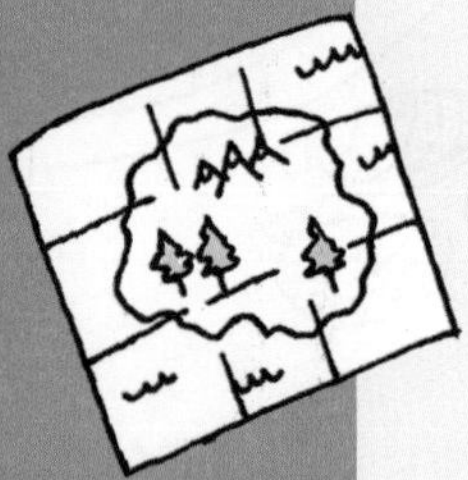
ma

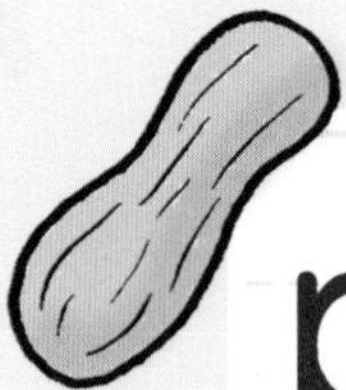
peanu

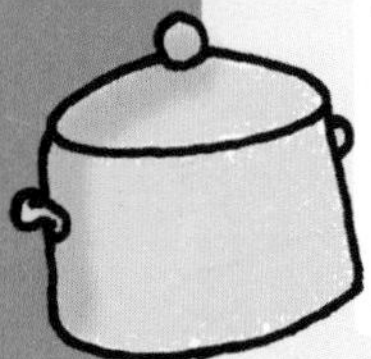
po

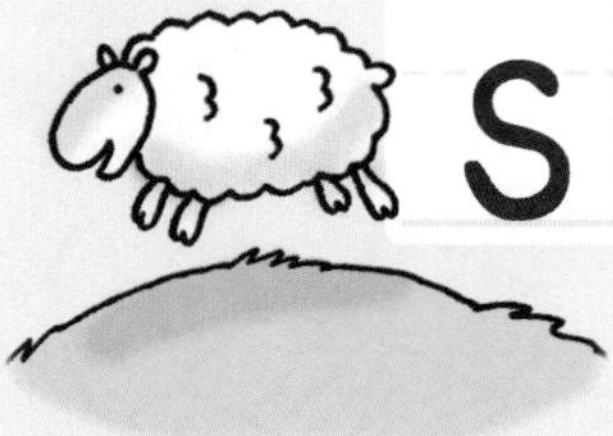
shee

Snail and Bus

The words for these pictures all end in **l** or **ll**, **s** or **ss**.

Say the word for each picture.

What ending sound do you hear?

Write the letter.

snai

bu

ba

gla

do

dre

she

plu

Frog and Duck

The words for these pictures all end in **g** or **k**.

Say the word for each picture.

Circle the pictures that end with a **g** sound.

Underline the pictures that end with a **k** sound.

Ending
consonants

Chicken Checkers!

Say the word for each picture.

Circle the pictures that begin with the **ch** sound.

BRAIN BOX

Sometimes two consonants that are next to each other make a new sound.

Example: **chip**

When you say **chip**, you don't hear the **c** and **h** sounds separately. You hear the new **ch** sound.

Show Me!

Say the word for each picture.

Circle the pictures that begin with the **sh** sound.

BRAIN BOX

Sometimes two consonants that are next to each other make a new sound.

Example: **shovel**

When you say **shovel**, you don't hear the s and h sounds separately. You hear the new **sh** sound.

The Theater!

Say the word for each picture.

Circle the pictures that begin with the **th** sound.

BRAIN BOX

Sometimes two consonants that are next to each other make a new sound.

Example: **theater**

When you say **theater**, you don't hear the **t** and **h** sounds separately. You hear the new **th** sound.

Short a

Say the word for each picture.

Color the cards with pictures that have the **short a** sound.

Short vowel sounds

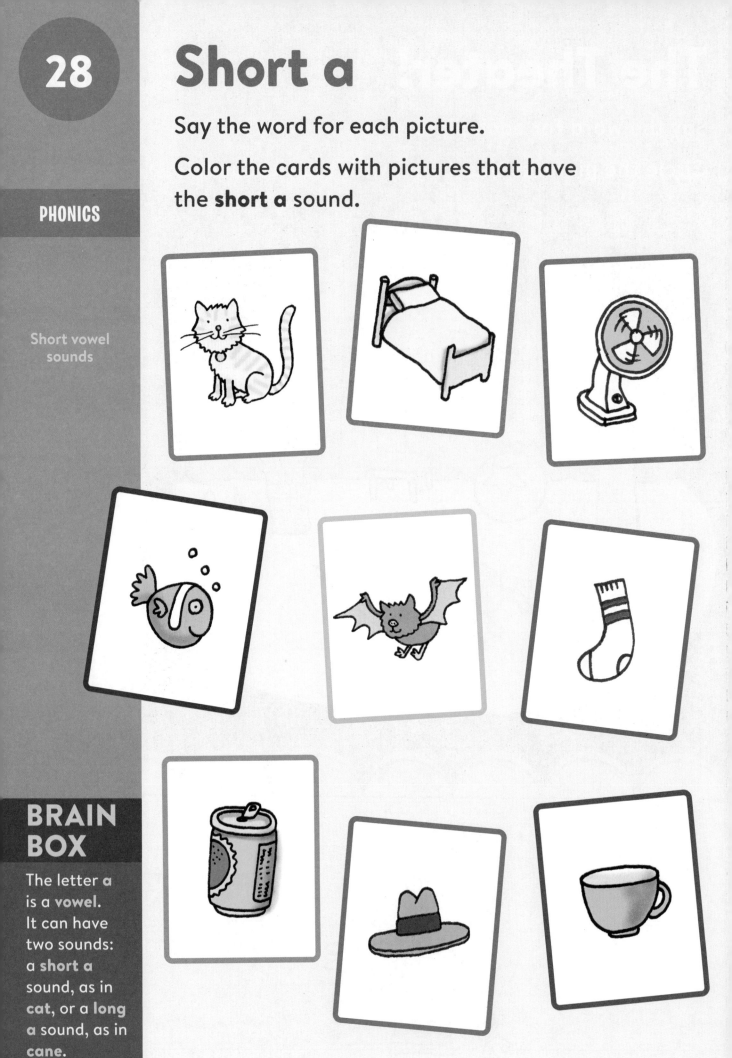

Short e

Say the word for each picture.

Color the cards with pictures that have
the **short e** sound.

Short vowel
sounds

BRAIN BOX

The letter e
is a **vowel.**
It can have
two sounds: a
short e sound,
as in **bed**, or a
long e sound,
as in **bee.**

Short i

Say the word for each picture.
Color the cards with pictures that have
the **short i** sound.

Short vowel
sounds

BRAIN BOX

The letter **i**
is a **vowel**.
It can have
two sounds: a
short i sound,
as in **fish**, or a
long i sound,
as in **bike**.

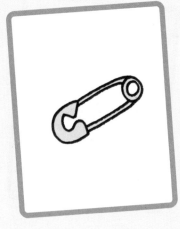

Short o

31

Say the word for each picture.
Color the cards with pictures that have
the **short o** sound.

Short vowel
sounds

BRAIN BOX

The letter o
is a **vowel**.
It can have
two sounds:
a **short o**
sound, as in
pot, or a **long**
o sound, as in
yo-yo.

Short u

Say the word for each picture.
Color the cards with pictures that have
the **short u** sound.

Short vowel
sounds

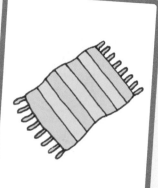

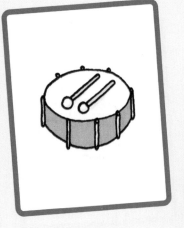

BRAIN BOX

The letter **u** is a **vowel**. It can have two sounds: a **short u** sound, as in **sun**, or a **long u** sound, as in **cube**.

Long a

Say the word for each picture.
Color the cards with pictures that have
the **long a** sound.

BRAIN BOX

The letter a
is a **vowel**.
It can have
two sounds:
a **short a**
sound, as in
cat, or a
long a sound,
as in **cane**.

Brain Quest Grade 1 Workbook

Long vowel sounds

Long e

Say the word for each picture.
Color the cards with pictures that have the **long e** sound.

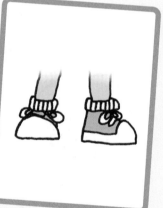

Long i

Say the word for each picture.
Color the cards with pictures that have
the **long i** sound.

Long vowel
sounds

BRAIN BOX

The letter **i**
is a **vowel.**
It can have
two sounds: a
short i sound,
as in **fish,** or a
long i sound,
as in **bike.**

Long o

Say the word for each picture.
Color the cards with pictures that have
the **long o** sound.

Long u

Say the word for each picture.
Color the cards with pictures that have
the **long u** sound.

Long vowel
sounds

BRAIN BOX

The letter u
is a **vowel**.
It can have
two sounds:
a **short u**
sound, as
in **sun**, or a
long u sound,
as in **cube**.

Long Vowel Review

Circle the word that has the same long vowel sound as the first word in that row.

| toe | ox | (hope) | read |

| hike | cube | big | time |

| rain | lake | seem | bat |

| bee | pen | look | heel |

| huge | but | cube | flea |

Jam and Cake

Say the word for each picture.

Draw a line from the pictures with the **short a** sound to the **jam**.

Draw a line from the pictures with the **long a** sound to the **cake**.

jam

cake

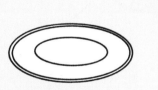

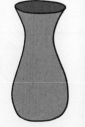

BRAIN BOX

The vowel a has two sounds: a **short a** sound, as in **jam**, or a **long a** sound, as in **cake**.

Short e
and long e

Red and Green

Say the word for each picture.

Draw a line from the pictures with the **short e** sound to the **red splash.**

Draw a line from the pictures with the **long e** sound to the **green splash.**

red

green

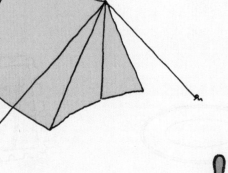

Jill and Mike

Say the word for each picture.

Draw a line from the pictures with the **short i** sound to **Jill**.

Draw a line from the pictures with the **long i** sound to **Mike**.

Jill

Mike

9

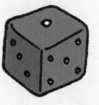

Milk

6

BRAIN BOX

The vowel i has two sounds: a **short i** sound, as in **Jill**, or a **long i** sound, as in **Mike**.

Fox and Goat

Say the word for each picture.

Draw a line from the pictures with the **short o** sound to the **fox**.

Draw a line from the pictures with the **long o** sound to the **goat**.

fox

goat

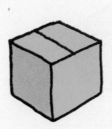

BRAIN BOX

The vowel o has two sounds: a **short o** sound, as in fox, or a **long o** sound, as in goat.

Sun and Moon

Say the word for each picture.

Draw a line from the pictures with the **short u** sound to the **sun**.

Draw a line from the pictures with the *loo/* sound to the **moon**.

sun

moon

Brain Quest Grade 1 Workbook

BRAIN BOX

The vowel **u** has different sounds including: a **short u** sound, as in **sun**, and an *loo/* sound, as in **blue**.

Fly and Monkey

Draw a line from the pictures that end with the **long i** sound to the **fly.**

Draw a line from the pictures that end with the **long e** sound to the **monkey.**

Words ending with y

fly

monkey

BRAIN BOX

The letter y can have two sounds: a **long i** sound, as in **fly**, or a **long e** sound, as in **monkey.**

SPELLING

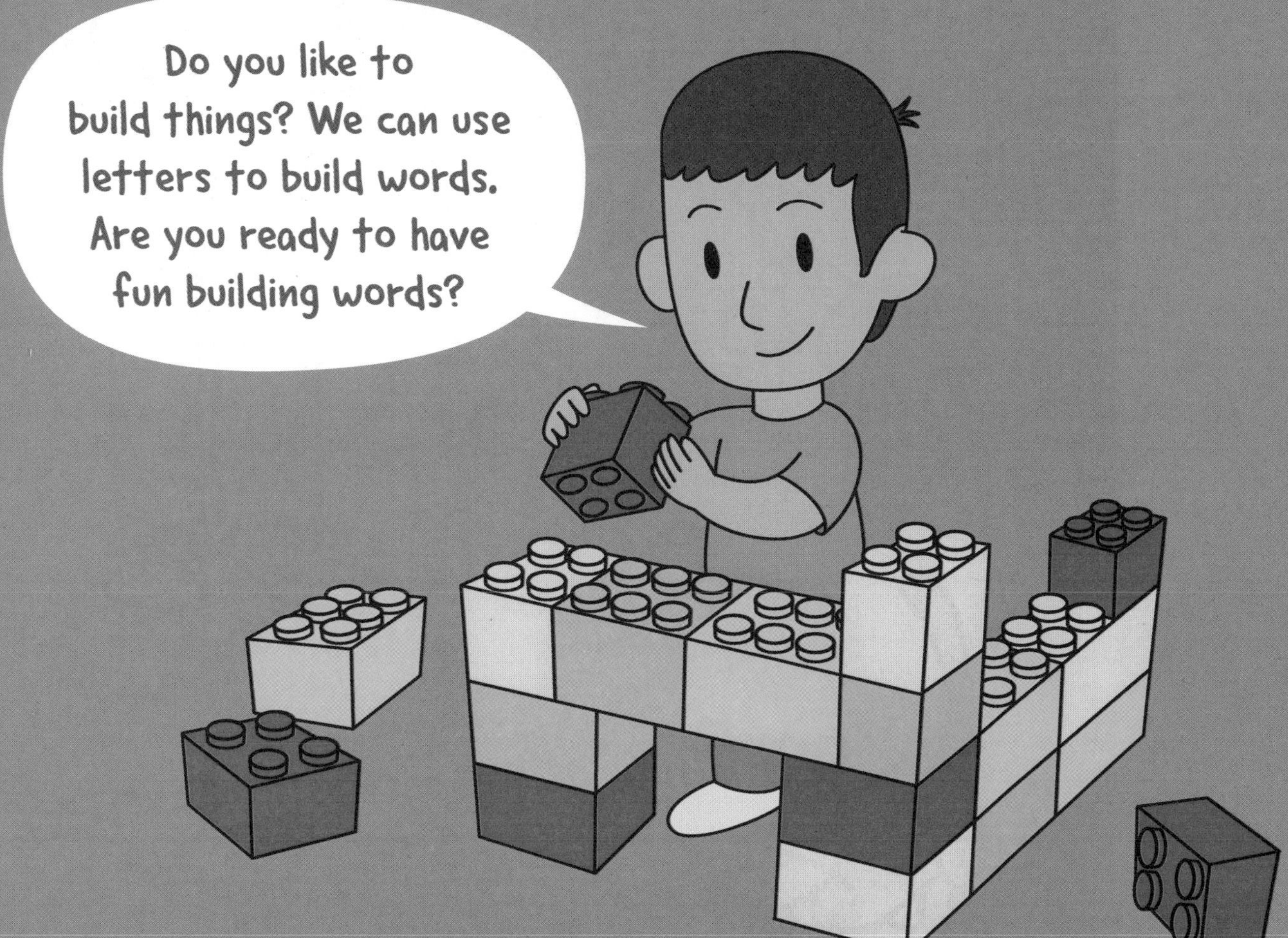

Do you like to
build things? We can use
letters to build words.
Are you ready to have
fun building words?

PARENTS Help develop your child's growth mindset. If your child says they can't do a task, point out that they just can't do it YET. This helps them understand that learning is a process and that they have the ability to learn challenging skills over time.

PLACE A STICKER HERE

For additional resources, visit www.BrainQuest.com/grade1

Animals! Animals!

Say the name for each animal.

Write the first letter to complete each word.

nake

og

at

rog

ird

ig

abbit

izard

urtle

Who Made the Mess?

Say the word for each picture.

Complete the words with consonants
from the clue list.

bo

bu

CLUES

k x p d g n s

boo

be

lam

do

cor

Whales and Snails

Complete each sentence with one of these **long a** words:

snail	rain	whale
paint	drain	plains

We want to ☐ the fence red.

Zebras roam the Kenyan ☐.

A  [ ] moves very slowly.

Water goes down the [ ].

The blue [ ] is the largest animal on Earth.

Hummingbirds drink drops of [ ].

Trees and Leaves

Complete each sentence with one of these **long e** words:

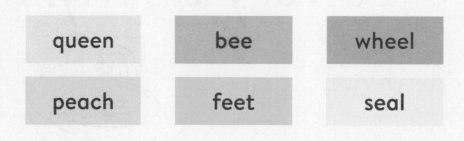

| queen | bee | wheel |
| peach | feet | seal |

Watch out!
That _____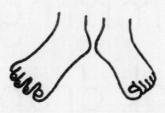
might sting you.

I have ten toes
on my _____.

The  plays in the waves.

My favorite dessert is _____ pie.

 The _____ wears a crown.

The _____ goes round and round.

A Day at the Park

Complete each sentence with one of these **long i** words:

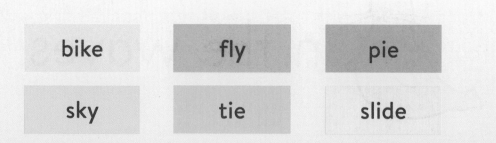

bike   fly   pie

sky   tie   slide

BRAIN BOX

Long i words can be spelled in different ways.

Some **long i** words are spelled with i_e, as in **mice**.

Some **long i** words are spelled with ie, as in **lie**.

And other **long i** words are spelled with y, as in **cry**.

Amy rides a ____.

Lori goes down the ____.

Rico eats the ____.

Cody wears a ____.

There are no clouds in the ____.

The ____ is buzzing around.

The bees live in a

_____

_____.

Long i words

Backyard Barbecue

Complete each sentence with one of these **long o** words:

toad	smoke	bone
cone	hose	boat

The kids are holding the [____].

A fire makes [_____].

Mom eats an ice cream [_____].

The dog has a [_____].

The [_____] jumps into the pool.

A [_____] floats in the water.

BRAIN BOX

Long o words can be spelled in different ways.

Some long o words are spelled with o_e, as in nose.

Some long o words are spelled with oa, as in goat.

Dude Ranch

Complete each sentence with one of these words that has the **/oo/ sound**:

blue	stool	tune
broom	tooth	boots

/oo/ sound

The cowboy _____ are blue.

Billy hums a _____.

The _____ jeans are worn by Billy.

The horse's big _____ sticks out of its mouth.

Ramón stands on a _____.

They use a _____ to sweep the ground.

/oo/ sound

BRAIN BOX

Words with /oo/ sounds can be spelled in different ways.

Some words with /oo/ sounds are spelled with oo, as in room.

Some words with /oo/ sounds are spelled with ue, as in clue.

Word Builders

Complete each word with one of the **r-blends** below:

SPELLING

R-blends

tr	fr	cr
br	gr	dr

__ oom

__ ab

__ og

__ uck

__ ape

__ um

BRAIN BOX

Blends are two consonants that go together. You can hear both letters in a blend.

Example: **drum**

Drum has an **r-blend**. When you say **drum**, you can hear both the **d** and the **r** sounds.

Slip and Slide

Complete each word with one of the **l-blends** below:

pl	gl	bl
sl	cl	pl

L-blends

 ide

 ane

 ack

 ant

 obe

 over

BRAIN BOX

Blends are two consonants that go together. You can hear both letters in a blend.

Example: **plane**

Plane has an **l-blend**. When you say **plane**, you can hear both the **p** and the **l** sounds.

Super S

Complete each word with one of the **s-blends** below:

S-blends

sn	sk	sp
sw	st	sm

ail

ar

ate

iral

ing

ile

BRAIN BOX

Blends are two consonants that go together. You can hear both letters in a blend.

Example: **snap**

Snap has an **s-blend**. When you say **snap**, you can hear both the **s** and the **n** sounds.

VOCABULARY

Can you name five colors? Five sports? Five animals? Knowing lots of words makes you a better reader and writer. Let's build our vocabulary!

PARENTS Making up silly rhymes and sharing tongue twisters are fun ways to play with words. Help grow your child's vocabulary by reading aloud a variety of texts and using rich language when you talk.

PLACE A STICKER HERE

For additional resources, visit www.BrainQuest.com/grade1

All About Mike

Read the words on the cards.

Write each word in the correct sentence.

am

and

I

you

I _____ Mike! _____ like to read _____ play.

What do _____ like to do?

is

see

my

run

This is ____ dog!

His name ____ Rex.

He likes to ____.

He must ____ a squirrel.

Where Is Everyone?

Read the words on the cards.

Write each word in the correct sentence.

Sight words

He

She

They

It

BRAIN BOX

We can use *he*, *she*, or *they* as a singular pronoun. Instead of writing "Sybil plays baseball," we can write "She plays baseball" OR "They play baseball." Both are correct.

Where is the boy?

_____ is on the swing.

Where is the girl?

_____ is on the slide.

Where is the ball?

_____ is under the tree.

Where are the twins?

_____ are on the

seesaw.

Where is Blake? _____

are jumping rope.

Team Up

Read the words on the cards.

Write each word in the correct sentence.

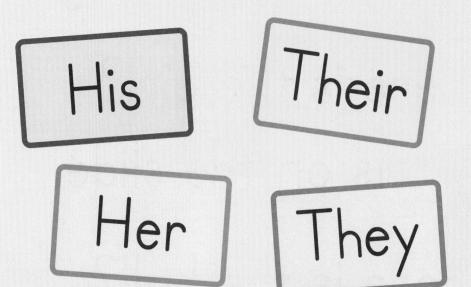

His   Their

Her   They

These are the Tigers.
They are a team.
_____ shirts are red.

This is Sue.

_____ shirt is orange.

This is Jack.

_____ shirt is green.

This is the coach.

_____ cheer on the team.

On the Farm

Read the words on the cards.

Write each word next to the correct animal.

cat

dog

cow

hen

horse

goat

duck

pig

Animal words

In the Kitchen

Read the words on the cards.

Draw a line from each card to the correct picture on the next page.

Kitchen words

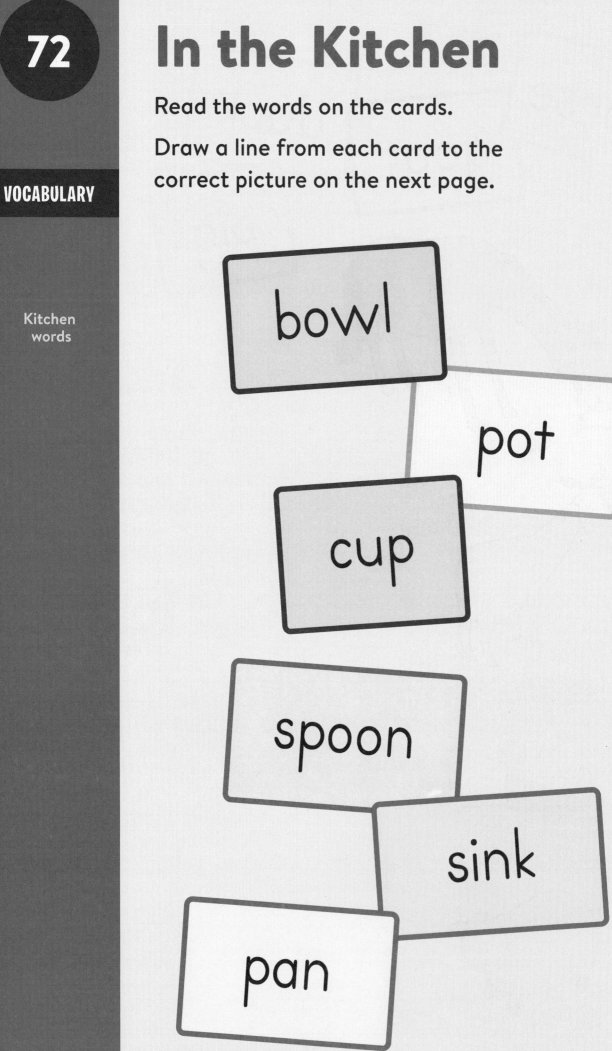

bowl

pot

cup

spoon

sink

pan

Food words

At the Farmers Market

Read the words on the cards.

Draw a line from each card to the correct food on the next page.

butter

pears

bread

cheese

apples

eggs

Food words

Color Splash!

Read the color words on the cards.

Color the card the right color.

Color words

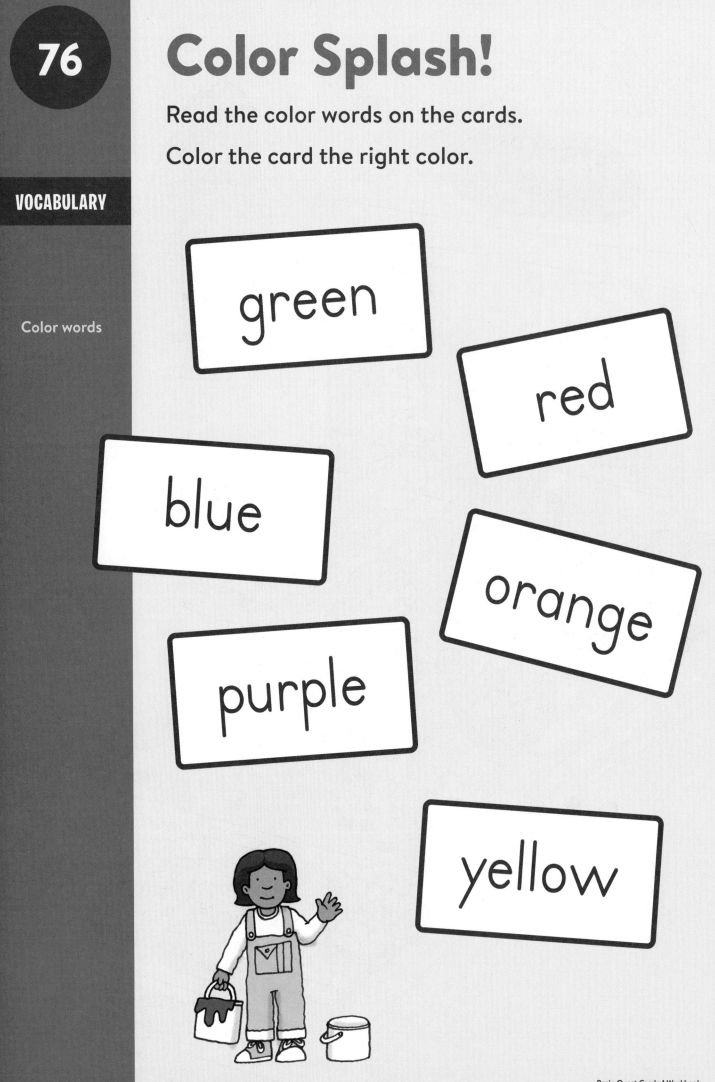

green

red

blue

orange

purple

yellow

Color words

Write the color word below each color.

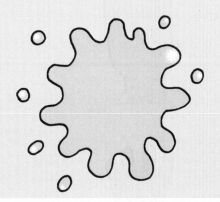

Finger Counting

Read the number words on the cards.

Count the number of fingers each hand is holding up.

Draw a line from each card to the correct hand.

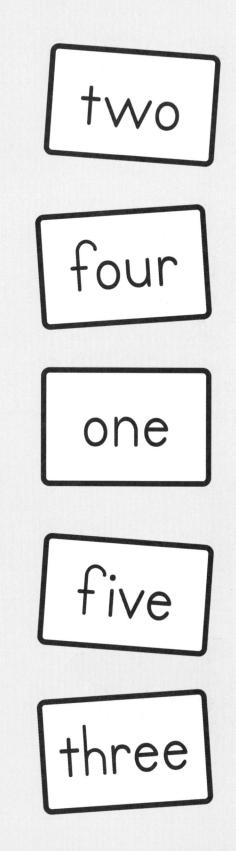

Number words

seven

nine

six

ten

eight

Activities!

Read the words on the cards.

Write each word in the correct sentence.

Action words

dance

sing

paint

read

I like to _____.

I like to _____.

We like to _____.

I like to _____.

Soccer Stars!

Read the words on the cards.

Write each word in the correct sentence.

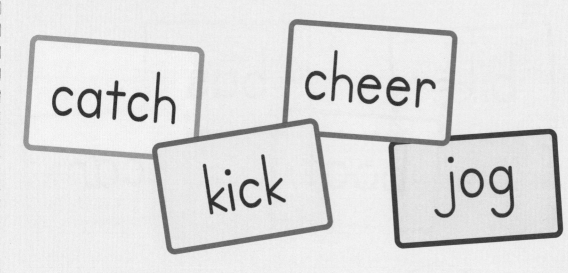

 We [_____] .

 We [_____] .

 We [_____] .

 We [_____] .

Let's Go!

Read the words on the cards.

Write each word next to the correct picture.

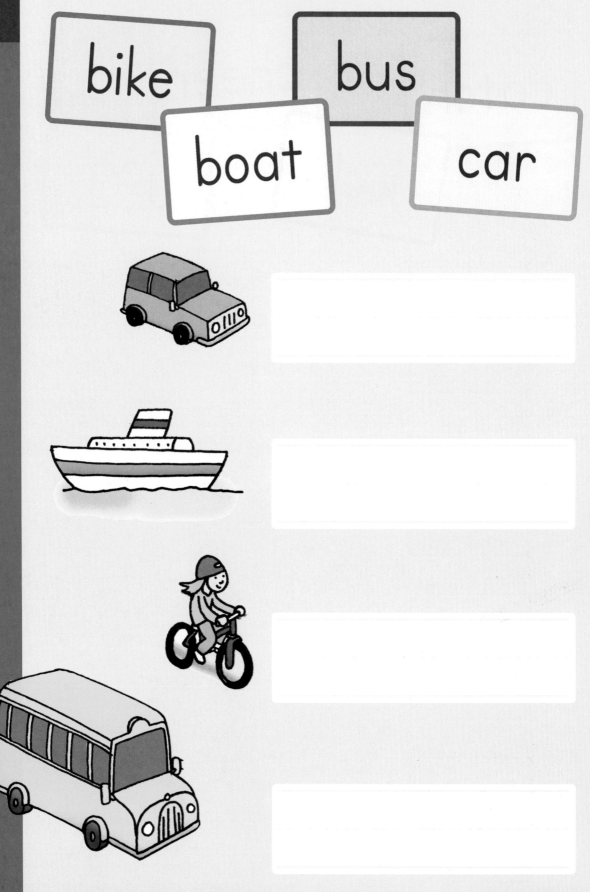

bike

bus

boat

car

VOCABULARY

Transportation words

plane train truck van

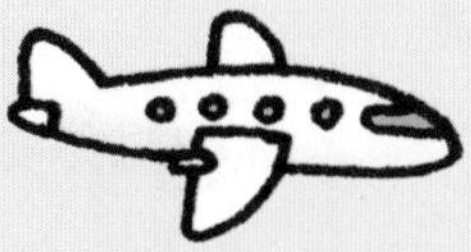

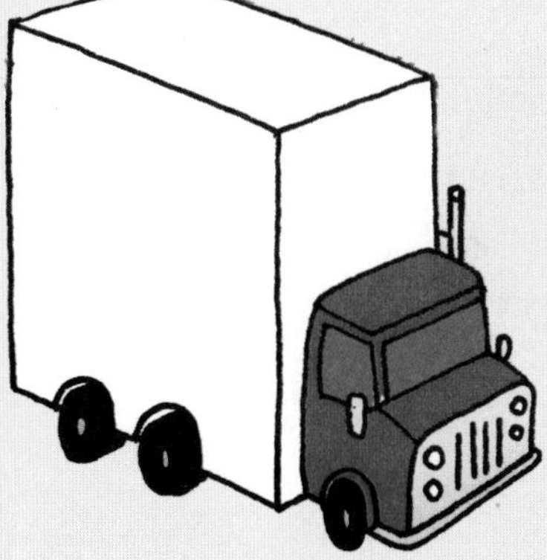

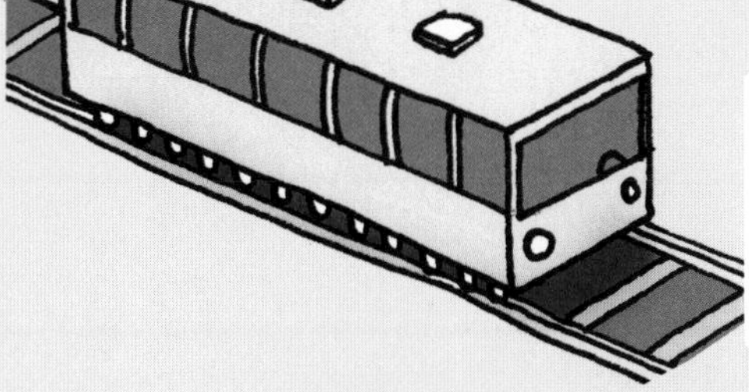

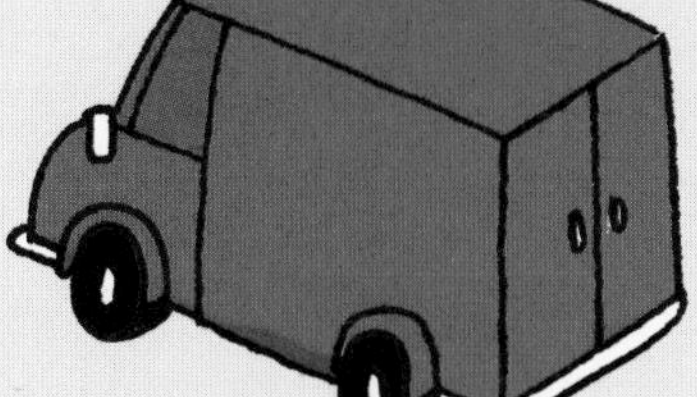

Time to Rhyme!

The words on the cards all rhyme with **brag**. Write each rhyming word next to the correct picture.

Rhyming words

tag

wag

bag

flag

BRAIN BOX

Rhyming words have the same middle and ending sounds.

Cat and **hat** are rhyming words.

The words on the cards all rhyme with **tan**.
Write each rhyming word next to the
correct picture.

pan

fan

can

man

Keep Rhyming!

The words on the cards all rhyme with **cool.**

Write each rhyming word under the correct picture.

Rhyming
words

school

pool

stool

spool

The words on the cards all rhyme with **tone**.

Write each rhyming word under the correct picture.

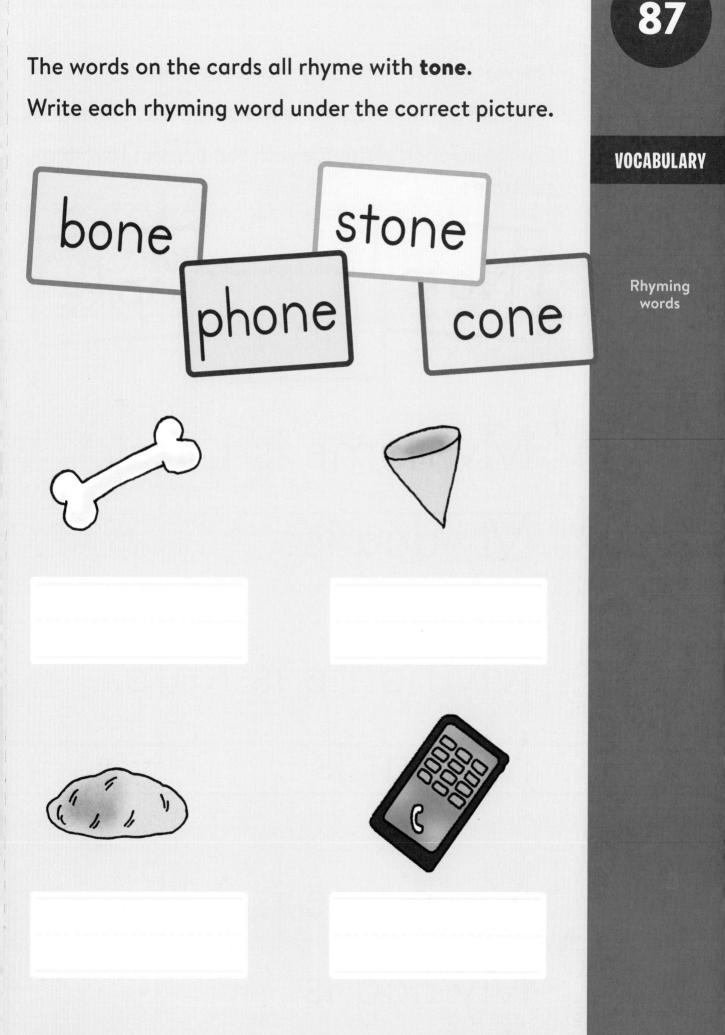

bone

stone

phone

cone

Our Pets

The words on the cards are the pet names.

Each pet's name rhymes with its owner's name.

Complete each sentence with the correct rhyming pet name.

Nate   Harry   Spike

My name is Larry.
My dog is _____.

My name is Kate.
My cat is _____.

My name is Mike.
My dog is _____.

Rhyming words

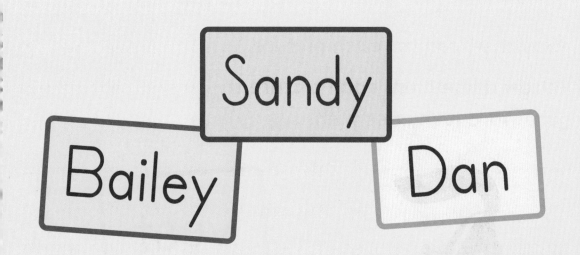

My name is Hailey.
My dog is _____ .

My name is Andy.
My cat is _____ .

My name is Jan.
My cat is _____ .

VOCABULARY

Rhyming words

Find the Rhyme

Say the word for each picture.

Draw a line from each picture to the word it rhymes with.

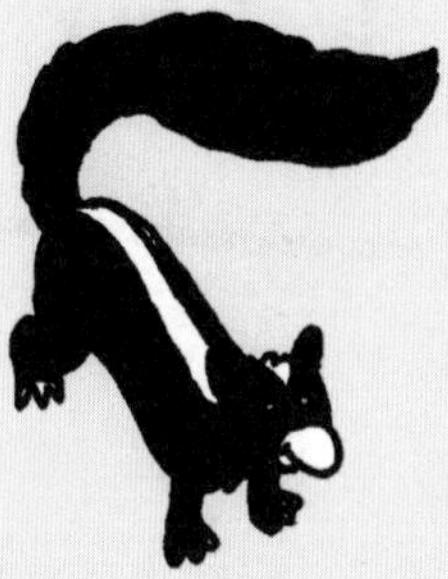

vest

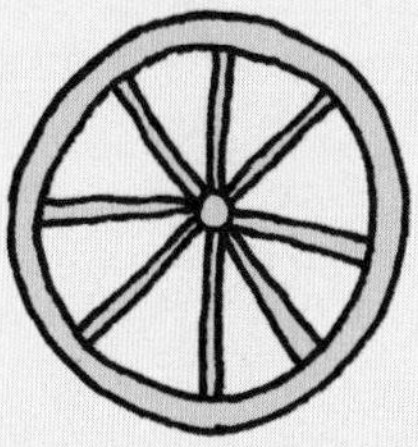

junk

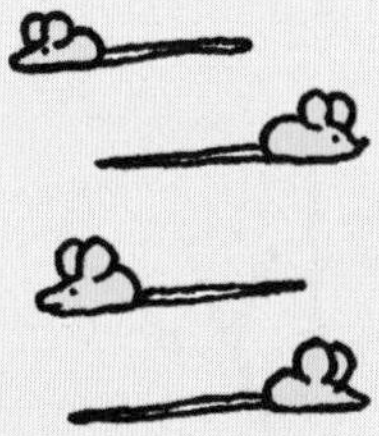

feel

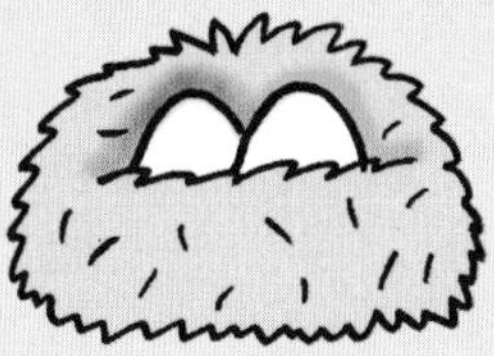

main

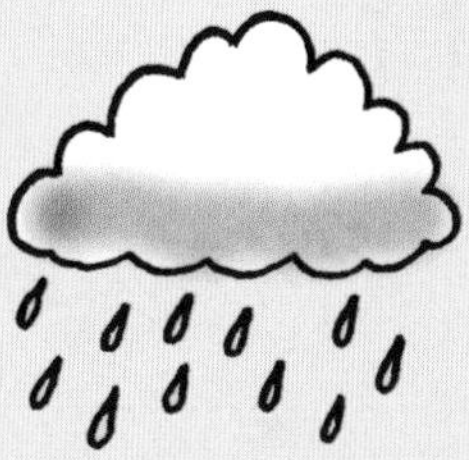

rice

LANGUAGE ARTS

There are different kinds of words—nouns, verbs, and adjectives—that we put together to make sentences. Are you ready to learn more about how words work?

PARENTS In this section, children practice reading, writing, and identifying the components of sentences, including the parts of speech and the features of statements and questions. Support your child by modeling correct grammar when reading books aloud and speaking with them.

PLACE A
STICKER
HERE

For additional resources, visit www.BrainQuest.com/grade1

People

Read the **nouns.**

They all name people.

Complete each sentence with the correct **noun** from the words below.

daughter   boy   woman

father   veterinarian

The _____
examines the cat.

The _____ is
wearing a brown sweater.

His _____
has pigtails.

The _____
has brown hair.

The _____
has a birdcage.

Nouns

Animals

Read the **nouns**.

They all name animals.

| turtle | cat | bird | dog |

Complete each sentence with the correct **noun** from page 94.

Nouns

The _____

chirps on a branch.

The _____

hides behind the bush.

The _____

walks on a leash.

The _____

rests on the rock.

Things

Read the **nouns**.

They all name things.

| hammer | nails | saw | wood |

BRAIN BOX

Words for things are **nouns**.

Complete each sentence with the correct **noun** from page 96.

José wants to build a birdhouse.

He has planks of

_____ .

He has a _____ to cut the wood.

He has a box of

_____ .

The _____ is next to his sister.

Places

Read the **nouns.**

They all name places.

| beach | city | farm |
| forest | lake | town |

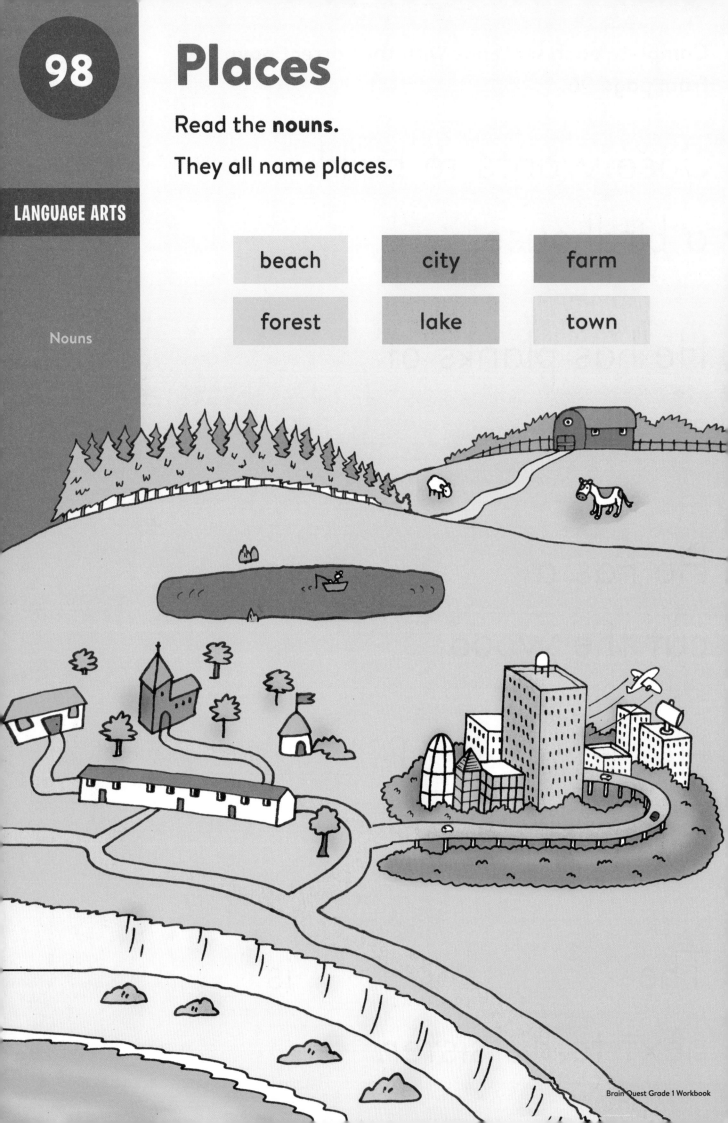

Complete each sentence with the correct **noun** from page 98.

We drive into _____.

The boat floats on the _____.

The cow lives on the _____.

There are tall buildings in the _____.

There is sand on the _____.

The _____ has lots of trees.

Go, Dino, Go!

Circle the **verb** in each sentence.

Verbs

The dinosaur eats.

The dinosaur hops.

The dinosaur runs.

BRAIN BOX

A **verb** is an action word. A **verb** tells what someone or something does.

Example: The dinosaur **sings**.

In this sentence, **sings** is the **verb**. It tells what the dinosaur does.

Verbs

The dinosaur hugs.

The dinosaur sleeps.

The dinosaur waves.

Naming Feelings

Read the adjectives.

Write the correct **adjective** next to each friend to describe how they are feeling.

happy	confused	shy

Adjectives

worried   proud   unhappy

Describe It!

Read the adjectives.

Write the correct **adjective** to tell about each animal.

| white | green | gray |

The _____ elephant lives in Kenya.

The _____ polar bear lives in the Arctic.

The _____ lizard lives in the desert.

| pink | brown | red |

The [ ] flamingo lives near the water.

The [ ] kangaroo lives in Australia.

The [ ] deer lives in the forest.

Cat Chase!

Read this sentence:

The cat naps.

Circle the **noun.**

Underline the **verb.**

Draw a box around the **capital letter** that begins the sentence.

Draw a triangle around the **period** that ends the sentence.

Now copy the **sentence** here.

_____

_____

BRAIN BOX

A **sentence** is a group of words that express a complete thought.

All sentences begin with a capital letter.

A **statement** is a sentence that explains or tells what someone or something does.

A statement ends with a period.

Circle the **noun** in this sentence:

The cat wakes up.

Underline the **verb** in this sentence:

The cat runs.

Draw a box around the **capital letter** that begins this sentence:

The dog chases the cat.

Draw a triangle around the **period** that ends this sentence:

The dog naps.

Superstar!

These sentences are written wrong.

Write each sentence correctly.

Statements

the cow sings.

The cow sings.

the cow dances

the cow acts

BRAIN BOX

A **statement** begins with a capital letter.

A **statement** ends with a period.

The receives
cow flowers.

Statements

cow bows. The

waves The cow

So Many Questions!

These questions are written wrong.

Write each sentence correctly.

how do you feel

___

who is your best friend

___

when is your next show

___

what is your favorite song

___

More Dessert, Please?

Read each question.

Circle the question word.

What kind of dessert is it?

Who made the dessert?

Where is the dessert?

When was the dessert ready?

Why did they make the dessert?

How does it taste?

Question words

BRAIN BOX

Questions start with question words.

Who, what, where, when, why, and how are all question words.

She Makes Pizza

Add the letter **s** to each verb to tell what is happening now.

Present-tense
verbs

She roll____ out the pizza dough.

She pour____ the sauce.

She sprinkle the cheese.

She put____ the pizza in the oven.

She take out the pizza.

BRAIN BOX

A **present-tense verb** tells what is happening now.

You can add the letter **s** to many verbs to tell about what is happening now.

They Planted Flowers!

Add the letters **ed** to each verb to tell what happened in the past.

They want [ ] to plant flowers.

Past-tense verbs

She gather [ ] the seeds.

He turn [ ] over the soil.

They pour [ ] the seeds in the ground.

BRAIN BOX

A **past-tense verb** tells what happened in the past.

You can add **ed** to many verbs to tell about actions that happened in the past.

He water [ ] the seeds.

The More the Merrier!

Look at the picture. Complete each sentence using the word **is** or **are**.

Is and are

Is and are

The monkeys climbing.

The elephant spraying.

The lions roaring.

The giraffe eating.

The zebra dancing.

The hippos singing.

Fresh Foods

Write the plural for each food word by adding the letter **s** at the end of the word.

Plural nouns

 pumpkin

pepper

carrot

 apple

BRAIN BOX

Plural means there is more than one.

You can add an **s** to make most nouns plural.

READING

What kinds of stories do you like to read? Are you ready to read stories about dragons, trees, robots, and more? Let's go!

PARENTS In this section, your child will improve their reading comprehension by practicing skills like sequencing, inferencing, and identifying text details. Have your child read the passages aloud and support them as needed.

PLACE A STICKER HERE

Drake the Dragon

Read about Drake.

Then answer the questions.

This is Drake.

Drake is a dragon.

Drake is purple.

Drake lives in a cave.

Drake lives with a snake.

Drake and the snake are best friends.

What is Drake?

Drake is a dragon .

What color is Drake?

Drake is _____ .

Where does Drake live?

Drake lives in a _____ .

Who is Drake's best friend?

Drake's best friend is a

_____ .

Picking Apples

Read about apples.

Then answer the questions.

Apples grow on trees.
You can pick apples in the fall.
This family is picking red apples.

Where do apples grow?

Apples grow on _____.

When can you pick apples?

You can pick apples in the

_____.

What color are the apples on the trees?

The apples are _____.

Camp Out

Read about the camping trip.

Number the pictures from 1 to 4 to show what happens in order.

1. We find a spot by the river.

2. We set up our tents.

3. We get some sticks for a fire.

4. We make dinner and sing!

Robot Race

Read about Robbie.

Then answer the questions.

> Robbie is a robot.
> Robbie is in a race.
> Robbie has wheels for feet!
> Robbie rolls fast.
> He rolls past the other robots.
> Robbie wins the race!

What is Robbie?

Robbie is a _____.

What does Robbie have for feet?

Robbie has _____.

Who wins the race?

_____

wins the race.

Draw your own robot here!

Understanding Feelings

Read the sentences.

Choose the correct word to tell how each person feels. Write it on the line.

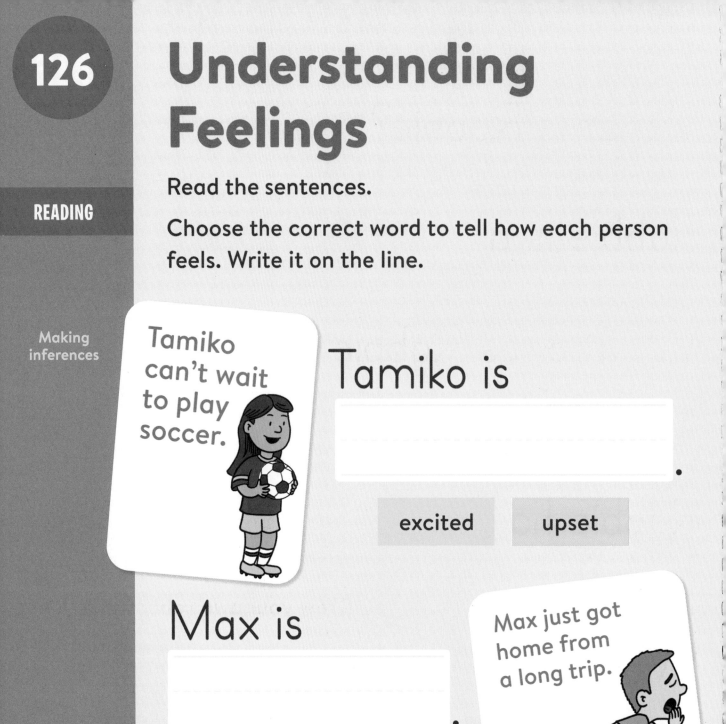

Tamiko can't wait to play soccer.

Tamiko is

excited   upset

Max is

sleepy   mad

Max just got home from a long trip.

Pilar is reading a book before bed.

Pilar is

sad   focused

Leo is a new student at school.

Leo is

_____ .

angry   nervous

Jamal is

_____ .

Jamal just found his lost dog!

happy   frustrated

Nora is

_____ .

Nora just won the school spelling bee!

proud   disappointed

Brain Quest Grade 1 Workbook

BRAIN BOX

Using specific words to explain our **emotions** helps us express how we are feeling. This builds our **emotional vocabulary** and allows us to be understood more clearly.

Plants!

Read about plants.

Flowers are plants.

Trees are plants.

Grass is a plant, too.

Rocks are not plants.

Water is not a plant.

The rabbit is not a plant.

Color the cards with plant words **green**.

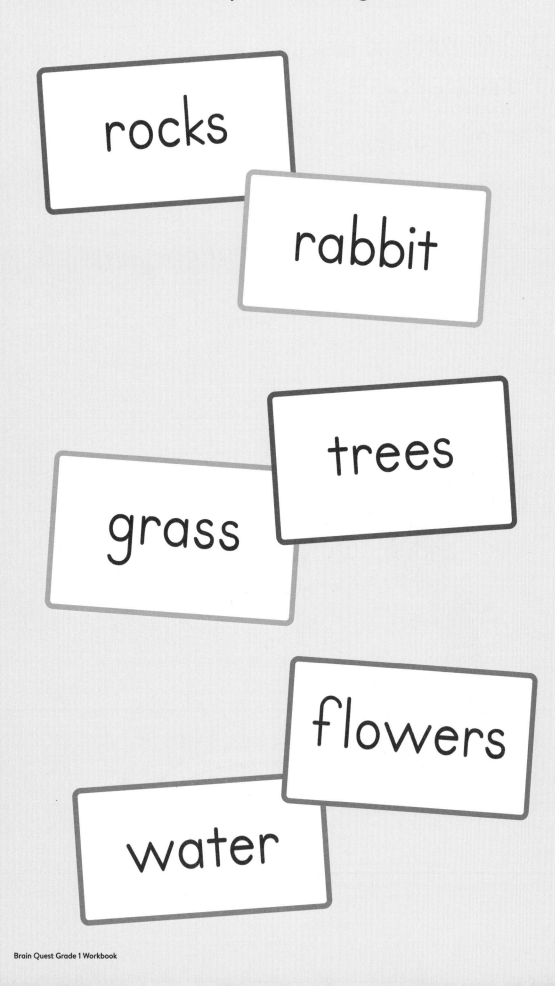

rocks

rabbit

trees

grass

flowers

water

Omar at the Beach

Omar went to the beach.

He saw sand.

He saw water.

He saw a crab.

He got hit by a wave. Omar got wet!

What did Omar see at the beach?

He saw sand.

Prior knowledge

Draw what you would pack for a day at the beach.

Monster Music!

Read each sentence.

Then draw a line to the matching picture.

Molly plays the drums.

Michael plays the tuba.

Mark plays the violin.

Maria plays the flute.

If you were a monster, what would you play?

I would play the

_____ .

Draw yourself playing your instrument.

The Witch's Spell

Read about the witch.

Number the pictures from 1 to 5 to show what happens in order.

1. Wilma the Witch has a frog.

2. She turns the frog into a bird!

3. She turns the bird into a bug!

4. She turns the bug into a dog!

5. She turns the dog into a frog again.

1

Sequencing

Duck's Day

Read about Duck.

Duck went for a walk.

It was a sunny day.

Duck felt a drop.

It began to rain!

That was okay.

Duck liked the rain.

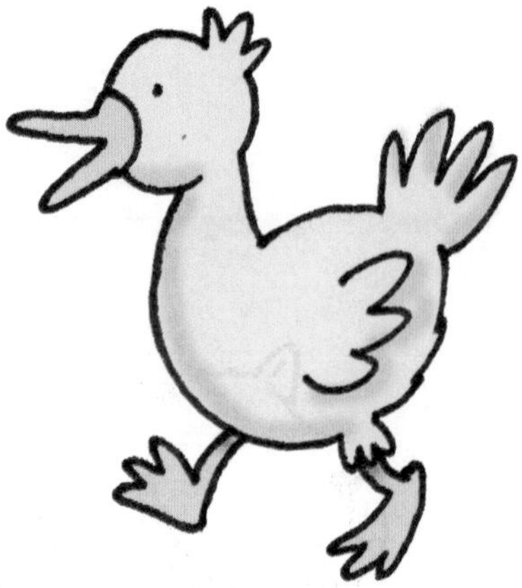

What do you predict Duck will do in the rain?

Draw a picture!

WRITING

We write to share our ideas. I like to write about my pet dog Boss. What do you like to write about?

PLACE A STICKER HERE

For additional resources, visit www.BrainQuest.com/grade1

Doggy Diary

WRITING

Sentence construction

Complete each sentence with a word below.

Then copy the whole sentence on the blank line.

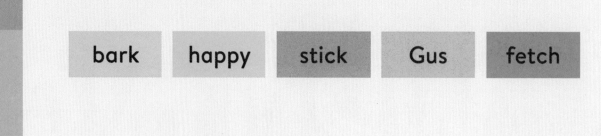

bark	happy	stick	Gus	fetch

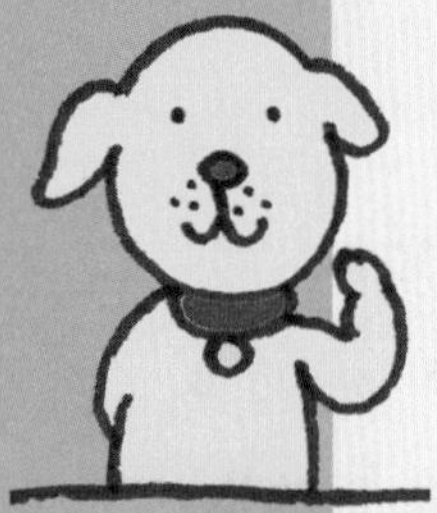

My name is ______.

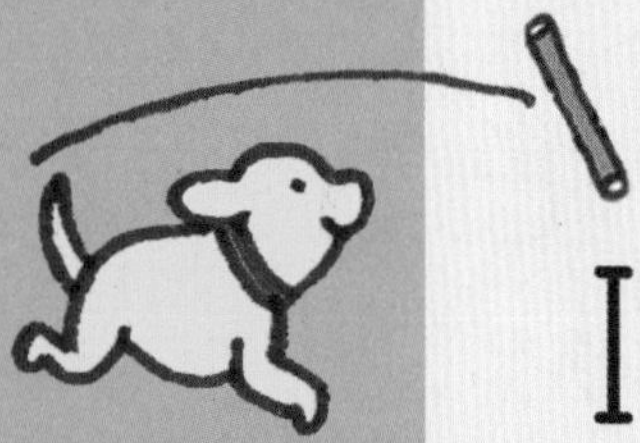

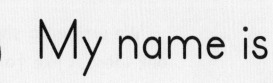

I like to ______.

Sentence construction

I fetch a _____ .

_____

_____ I like to _____ .

_____

I am a _____ dog.

_____

All About You!

Complete each sentence with a word that tells about you. Then copy the whole sentence on the blank line.

My name is _____ .

_____

I like
the color _____ .

_____

My favorite animal is
a/an _____ .

_____

Now draw a picture of yourself wearing your favorite color and playing with your favorite animal.

Sentence construction

Playing at the Pond

Write a sentence about each animal you see at the pond. Begin each sentence with **I see a.**

frog

fox

duck

I see a duck.

Statements

deer

fish

turtle

BRAIN BOX

A **statement** is a sentence that explains or tells what someone or something does.

A statement begins with a capital letter and ends with a period.

Let's Ride!

Write a sentence about each way to ride.

Begin each sentence with **I ride in a.**

boat

car

I ride in a car.

plane

train

Statements

wagon

Silly Pig!

Complete each sentence with the correct word from below.

Then copy the whole sentence on the blank line.

Sentence construction

| silly | sad | angry |

The pig is _____.

_____

| house | tree | mud |

The pig rolls in _____.

_____

| runs | dances | sits |

The pig _____.

_____

Sentence
construction

eats   sleeps   sings

The pig _____ .

_____

dog   cat   girl

The pig likes the _____ .

_____

ice cream   pizza   cookies

They eat _____ .

_____

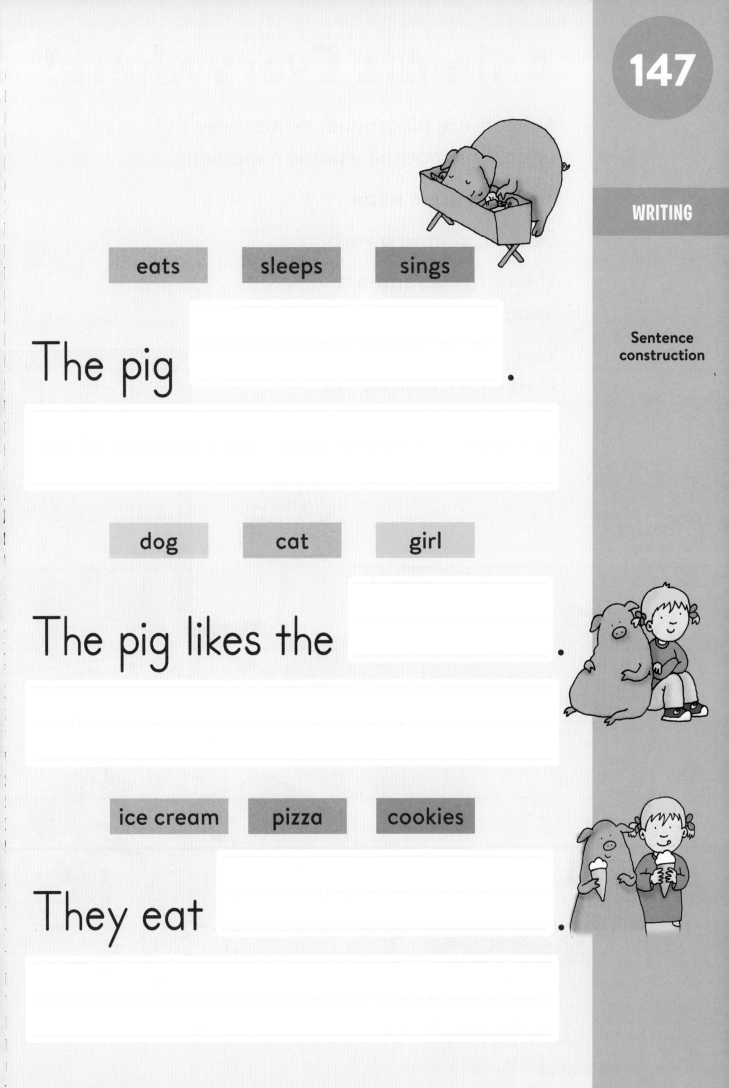

Animals Everywhere!

Animals are all around. Write three sentences that tell what is happening.

First, choose a **noun**.

Second, choose a **verb**.

Then write a sentence using both words.

Your sentence should start with the word **The**.

BRAIN BOX

A **noun** is a word that names a person, a place, or a thing.

A **verb** is an action word. A **verb** tells what someone or something does.

NOUNS
dog
cat
bird
bunny
child

VERBS
hops
runs
barks
sings
eats

The child runs.

Growing a Garden

Write two sentences that tell about the garden.

First, choose a **noun**.

Then choose an **adjective**.

Now write a sentence using both words.

Your sentence should start with the word **The**.

Describing
sentences

BRAIN BOX

Adjectives are words that describe a person, place, or thing.

Example:
The ball is **blue**.

The word **blue** is an adjective. It describes the **ball**.

Describing
sentences

NOUNS
carrot
corn
cucumber
pumpkin
tomato

ADJECTIVES
big
orange
green
red
tall

The pumpkin
is big.

Monster Mash

Write four sentences about Monster.

Use a **verb**, an **adjective**, and a **noun** for each sentence.

Start each sentence with **Monster**.

VERBS
eats
throws
licks
drinks

ADJECTIVES
red
spooky
funny
green

NOUNS
bugs
balls
candy
slime

Monster eats
red bugs.

Creative
writing

At the Dog Park

Write a sentence about each dog.

Use a **noun**, a **verb**, and an **adjective** in each sentence.

Creative writing

BRAIN BOX

Remember: Sentences start with **capital letters** and end in **periods, question marks,** or **exclamation marks.**

Creative
writing

Creative
writing

What Do You See?

Look around the room. Draw something you see in
the box.

Think of words that tell about your picture.

Write two sentences about your picture
using these words.

SEQUENCING AND SORTING

Step 1, step 2, step 3— you're probably great at following directions. Putting things in order is like following directions. Let's practice!

PARENTS This section features visual exercises that bridge language development, math, and technology. Look for opportunities to extend this conversation during other activities by asking questions like: What happened first? What do you think will happen next? What happened at the end?

PLACE A STICKER HERE

Up, Up, and Away!

Number the pictures from 1 to 4 to show what happens in order.

Sequencing

1

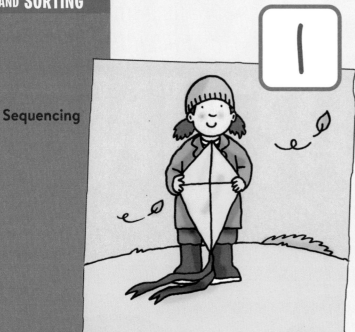

Welcome to the Club!

Number the pictures from 1 to 4 to show what happens in order.

Sequencing

Dog Wash

Number the pictures from 1 to 4 to show what happens in order.

Sequencing

Lunchtime!

Number the pictures from 1 to 6 to show what happens in order.

A Chick Is Born

Draw a line from each picture to the correct number to show what happens in order.

Sequencing

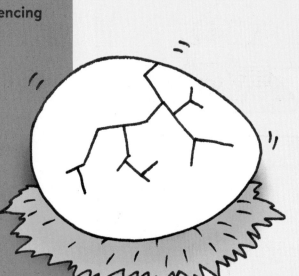

1　　**2**　　**3**

4   5   6

Growing Tall!

Draw a line from each picture to the correct number to show what happens in order.

Sequencing

1

2

3

4

5

6

Search and Sort

Look at the **numbers** in the clouds.

Write them in **numerical order** below the balloon.

Sorting

_____

Look at the **letters** in the clouds.

Write them in **alphabetical order** below the balloon.

Sorting

t

p

a

z

i

LETTERS

168# Fun in the Snow

Look at each picture.

What happens next?

Finish the snowman for the kids.

168SEQUENCING AND SORTING

Sequencing and sorting

168Brain Quest Grade 1 Workbook

MATH SKILLS

We think about numbers all the time! I'm thinking: How many cookies are on these plates? Which plate has more? Are you ready to think about numbers too?

PARENTS In first grade, kids learn to think critically and flexibly about numbers by skip counting, estimating, and considering place value. Practice by skip counting by 2s, 5s, and 10s forward and backward or by estimating the number of items on a plate and then counting to check your guess.

For additional resources, visit www.BrainQuest.com/grade1

Moving Day

Draw a line from the box to the matching number of things.

Number recognition

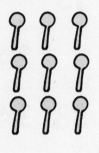

Count Dracula!

Fill in the missing numbers.

Count across and write the missing numbers in order.

Counting to 100

1		3	4			7	8	9	
	12	13			16			19	
21	22		24			27	28		
	33	34	35	36	37				40
	42			45			48	49	
51	52	53	54				58		60
	62			66	67		69		
71		73		75		77		79	
81	82	83					88		
	92		95		97				

Counting Crayons

Write the number of crayons below each group.

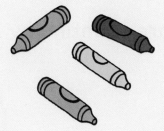

Now say the numbers out loud.

You are counting by 2s!

Brain Quest Grade 1 Workbook

Counting Fish

Write the number of fish below each group.

Say the numbers out loud.

You are counting by 2s!

Orange Trees

Write the number of oranges below each tree.

Say the numbers out loud.

You are counting by 5s!

At the Market

Write the number of things below each group.

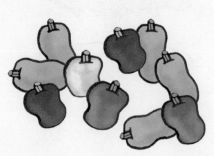

How many foods are there in all? Skip count by 10s to find out! Fill in the missing numbers.

| 10 | 20 | | 40 | |
| 60 | | | 90 | |

Number Value

Look at each number. Write each number as tens and ones on the **place value** chart.

MATH SKILLS

Place value

	tens	ones
35	3	5
47		
26		
82		
73		
19		
66		

BRAIN BOX

Place value tells us the value of each numeral. Look at the number 25.

The **2** tells us there are **2** tens. The **5** tells us there are **5** ones.

tens	ones
2	5

Tens and Ones

Look at each number.

Then answer the questions.

Place value

23 How many tens? __2__ ones? __3__

16 How many tens? _____ ones? _____

67 How many tens? _____ ones? _____

49 How many tens? _____ ones? _____

91 How many tens? _____ ones? _____

38 How many tens? _____ ones? _____

84 How many tens? _____ ones? _____

Bouncy Balls

Count the groups of balls.
Write the numbers of tens and ones in the boxes.
Write the total number of balls in the circle.

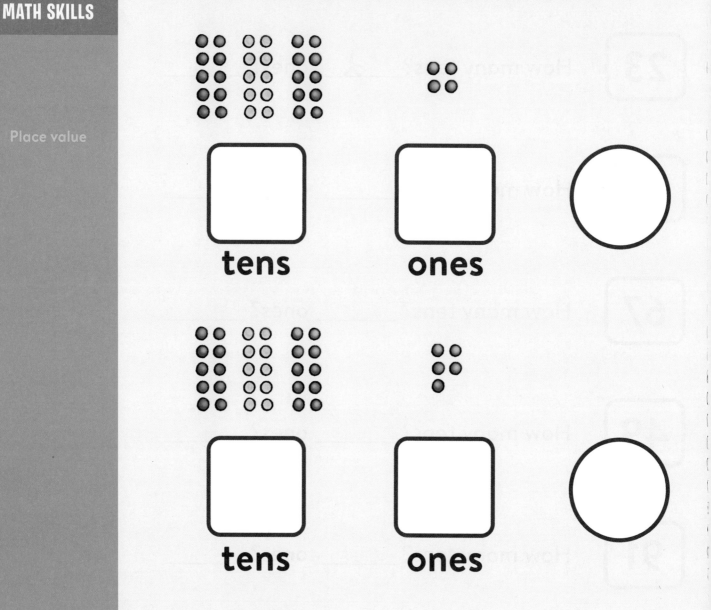

tens   ones

tens   ones

BRAIN BOX

Some numbers, like 38, have two digits. The number **38** is made of **3** tens and **8** ones.

tens	ones
3	**8**

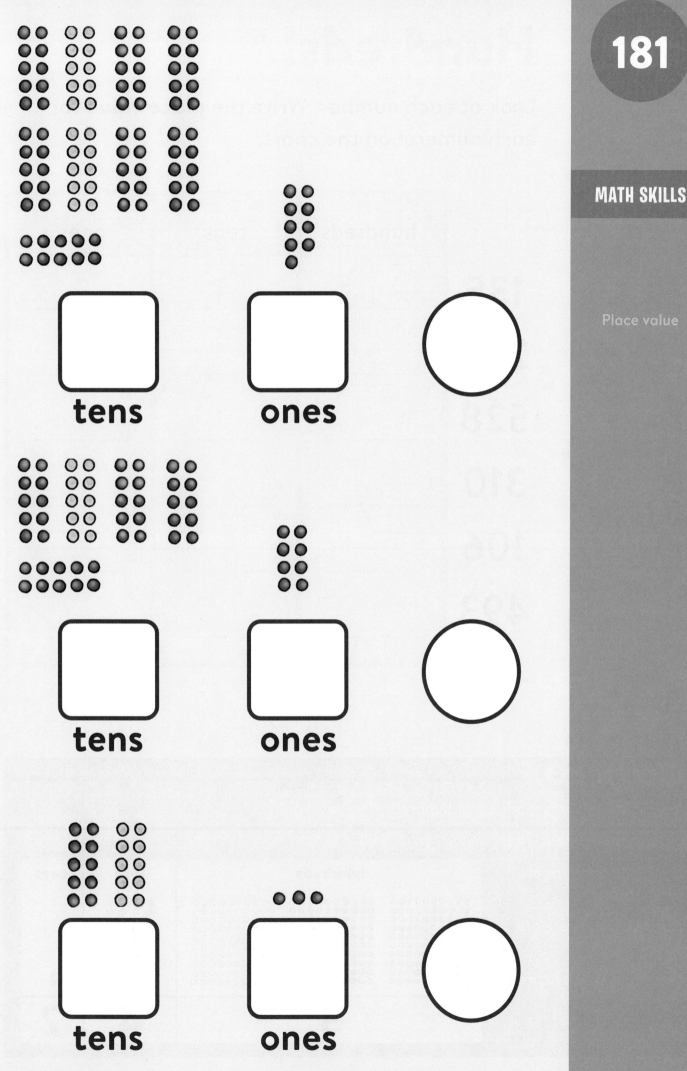

tens · ones · ○

tens · ones · ○

tens · ones · ○

Hundreds!

Look at each number. Write the **place value** for each numeral on the chart.

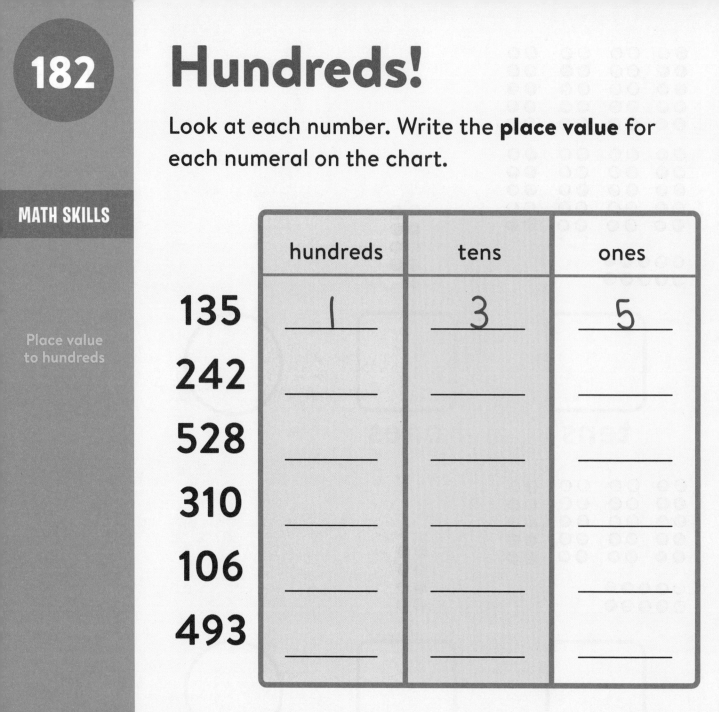

	hundreds	tens	ones
135	1	3	5
242	___	___	___
528	___	___	___
310	___	___	___
106	___	___	___
493	___	___	___

BRAIN BOX

A 3-digit number is made up of hundreds, tens, and ones.

Look at the number **342**.

The **3** tells us there are **3** hundreds.

The **4** tells us there are **4** tens.

The **2** tells us there are **2** ones.

hundreds	tens	ones
3	4	2

You're a Star!

Count the stars on each card. Color the card that has more stars.

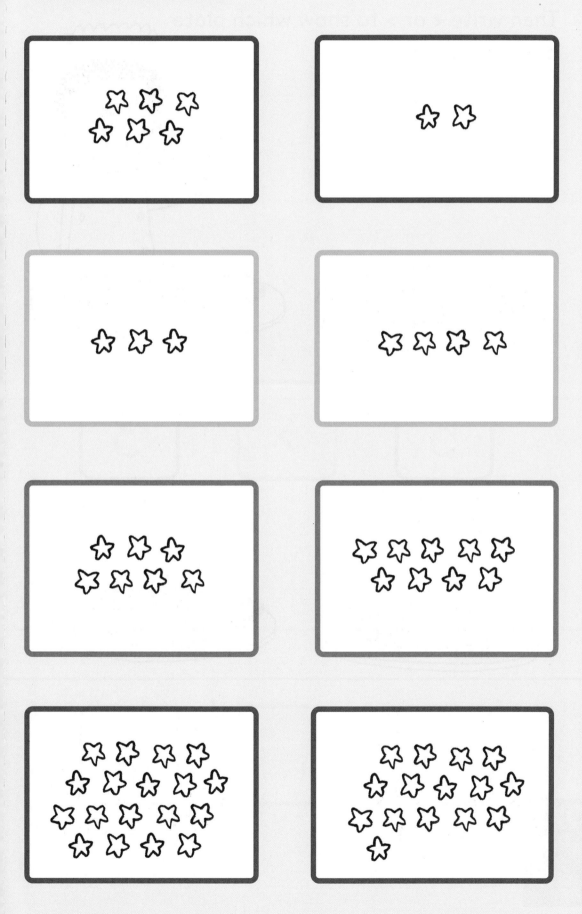

Bake Sale

Count the brownies on each plate.
Write the number in the box below the brownies.
Then write **<** or **>** to show which plate
has more brownies.

5 > 3

☐ ☐ ☐

BRAIN BOX

< means **less than.**

> means **greater than.**

Greater than, less than

Brick by Brick

Look at the brick towers.

Circle the tower with the **most** bricks.

Put an X on the tower with the **fewest** bricks.

Circle the towers with the **same number** of bricks.

Put an X on the tower with the **fewest** bricks.

Comparing
numbers

Circle the tower with the **most** bricks.

Put an X on the tower with the **fewest** bricks.

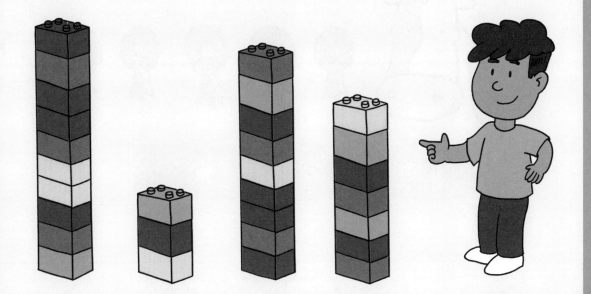

Circle the towers with the **same number** of bricks.

Put an X on the tower with the **fewest** bricks.

Award Winners!

For each ribbon, color a block on the bar.

Circle the animal that won the most ribbons.

Graphs

Book Worm

How many books do you think you see?

Don't count them. Just take a guess!

Write the number
you guessed:

Good job! You **estimated**!

Now count the books.
Write the number you counted:

Were you close?

Pot of Gold

How many gold coins do you think you see?

Don't count them. Just take a guess!

Write the number you guessed:

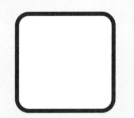

Good job! You estimated!

Now count the coins.

Write the number you counted:

Were you close?

Snow Day!

How many snowflakes do you think you see?
Don't count them. Just take a guess!

Write the number you guessed:

Now count the snowflakes.
Write the number you counted:
Were you close?

ADDITION AND SUBTRACTION

When we add, we bring numbers together to make a new total. When we subtract, we take one number away from another. Let's practice adding and subtracting.

PARENTS Support and reinforce the concepts in this section by asking your child about adding and subtracting throughout the day—for example, at the grocery store (how many items are in our cart?), in the kitchen (how many eggs are left if I take 1 away?), or at bedtime (how many stuffed animals are there altogether?).

PLACE A STICKER HERE

For additional resources, visit www.BrainQuest.com/grade1

Addition

Play Ball!

Count the balls in each group.

Write the number in the box below.

Write the **sum** in the colored box.

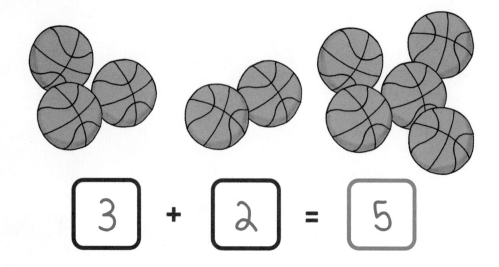

$$\boxed{3} + \boxed{2} = \boxed{5}$$

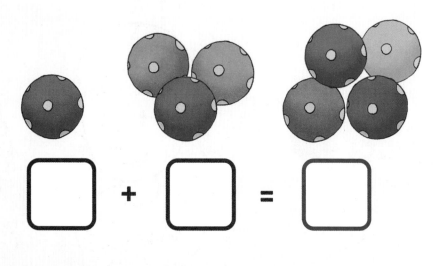

$$\boxed{} + \boxed{} = \boxed{}$$

 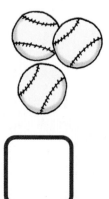

$$\boxed{} = \boxed{} + \boxed{}$$

Star Search

Count the stars in each group.

Write the number in the box below.

Write the **sum** in the colored box.

Addition

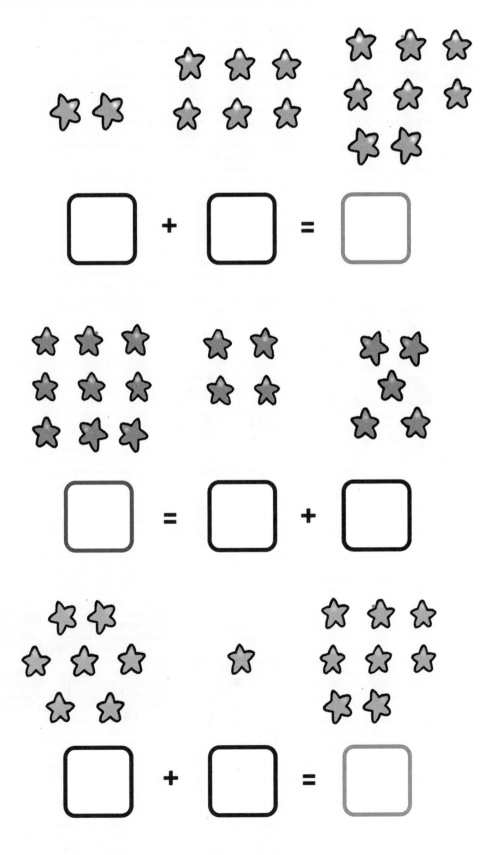

At the Toy Store

Count the toys in each group.

Write the number in the box below.

Add the numbers. Write the **sum** in the colored box.

Addition

$$5 + 3 = 8$$

Addition

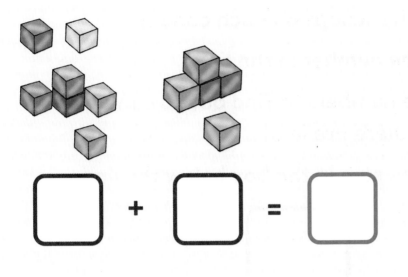

□ + □ = □

□ = □ + □

□ + □ = □

Super Scoops!

Count the scoops on each cone.

Write the number in the box.

Add the numbers to find out how many scoops there are in all.

Write the **sum** in the box below the line.

Addition

+

 +

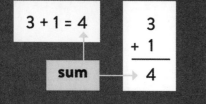

Pancake Party!

Count the pancakes on each plate.

Write each number in the box.

Add the numbers to find out how many pancakes there are in all.

Write the **sum** in the box below the line.

Addition

$+$

$+$

So Many Shells!

Count the shells in each group.

Add the shells.

Draw a line to the correct answer.

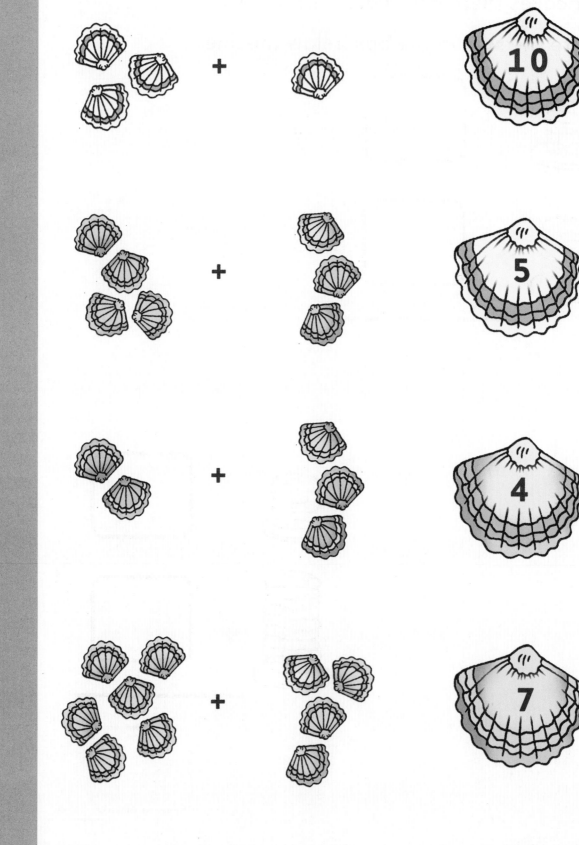

Monster Math

Add the numbers in the boxes.

Write the **sum** in the box.

Addition

3 + 5 = 8

2 + 4 = ☐

8 + 1 = ☐

2 + 3 = ☐

☐ = 6 + 1

Dragon Math

Add the numbers.

Write the **sum** in each box.

Addition

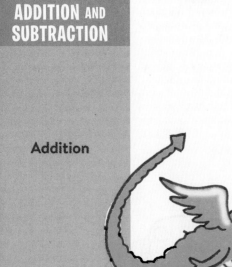

$5 + 2 = $ ☐

$4 + 8 = $ ☐

$1 + 9 = $ ☐

☐ $= 2 + 8$

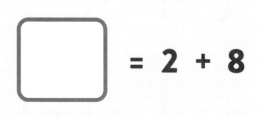

6	3	6	2
+ 1	+ 5	+ 4	+ 4
☐	☐	☐	☐

Addition

[ ] = 1 + 6

[ ] = 7 + 5

2 + 7 = [ ]

8 + 4 = [ ]

5 + 6 = [ ]

7 + 6 = [ ]

[ ] = 9 + 5

[ ] = 10 + 3

4 + 3 = [ ]

5 + 5 = [ ]

$$\begin{array}{r} 4 \\ + 2 \\ \hline \end{array}$$ [ ]

$$\begin{array}{r} 5 \\ + 7 \\ \hline \end{array}$$ [ ]

$$\begin{array}{r} 11 \\ + 4 \\ \hline \end{array}$$ [ ]

$$\begin{array}{r} 4 \\ + 7 \\ \hline \end{array}$$ [ ]

Bear Numbers

Add the numbers.

Write the **sum** in each box.

Addition

6 + 4 = ☐

3 + 2 = ☐

7 + 7 = ☐   4 + 1 = ☐

☐ = 2 + 6   ☐ = 5 + 4

5	3	2	8
+ 12	+ 7	+ 9	+ 1
☐	☐	☐	☐

Addition

3 + 2 = [ ]

[ ] = 8 + 4

4 + 7 = [ ]

2 + 10 = [ ]

[ ] = 7 + 2

4 + 10 = [ ]

3 + 9 = [ ]

5 + 6 = [ ]

9 + 2 = [ ]

[ ] = 10 + 4

```
  6        5        3        1
+ 2      + 3      + 9      + 8
-----    -----    -----    -----
[   ]    [   ]    [   ]    [   ]
```

Terrific 20!

Count the insects in each group.

Write the number in the box below.

Add the numbers.

Write the **sum** in the box.

Adding to 20

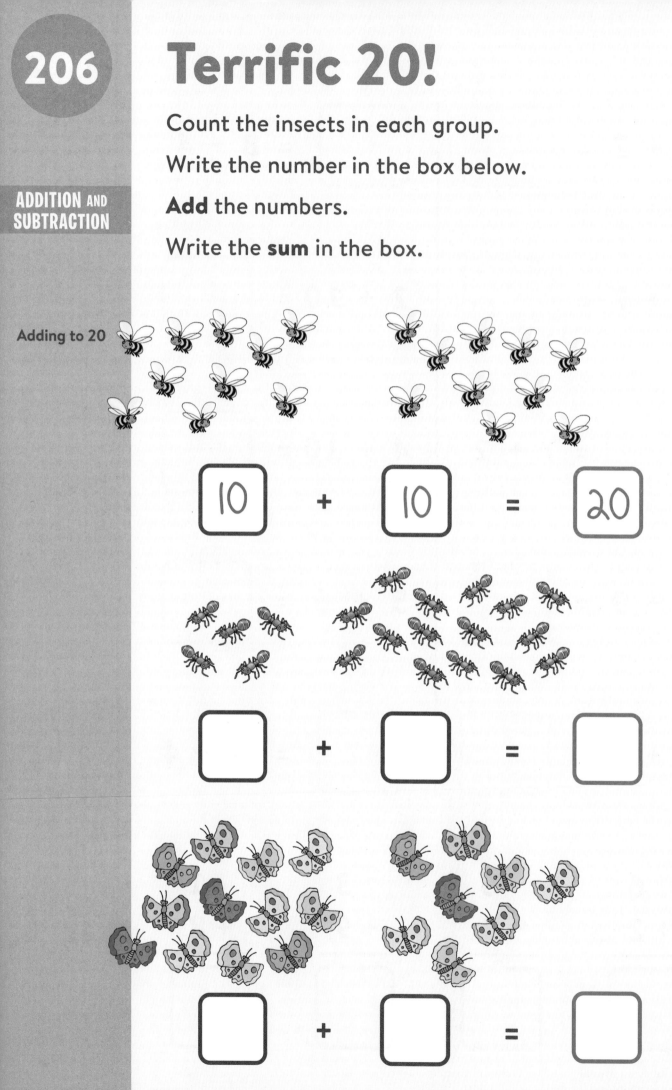

10 + 10 = 20

☐ + ☐ = ☐

☐ + ☐ = ☐

Adding to 20

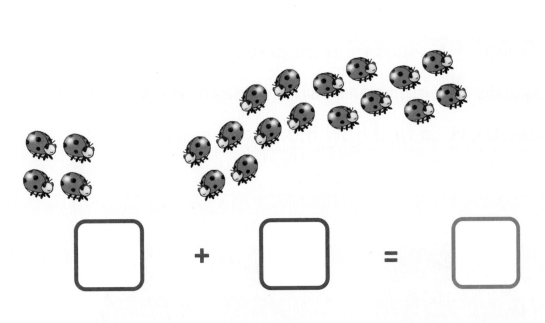

$\boxed{}$ + $\boxed{}$ = $\boxed{}$

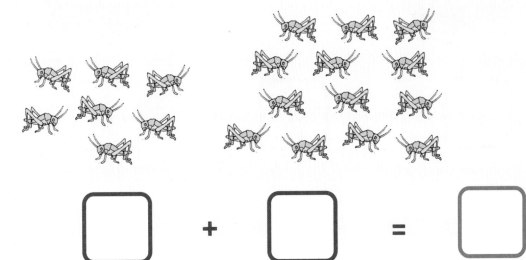

$\boxed{}$ + $\boxed{}$ = $\boxed{}$

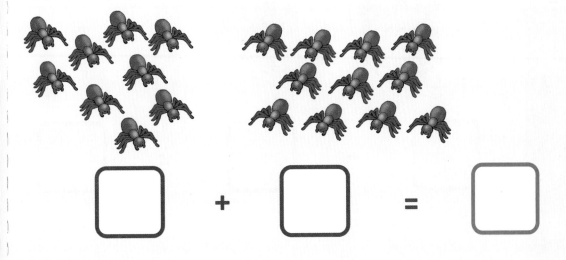

$\boxed{}$ + $\boxed{}$ = $\boxed{}$

Subtraction

Take a Slice!

Count the slices in each pizza.

Count the number of slices taken away.

Subtract to find how many slices are left.

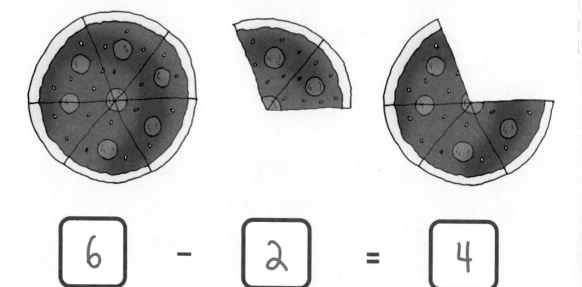

$$\boxed{6} - \boxed{2} = \boxed{4}$$

BRAIN BOX

To **subtract**, you take away.

Example:
3 − 2 = 1

Here, we are subtracting the number **2** from the number **3**. We use a − sign to show subtraction.

1 is how many we have left. This is called the **difference**. The amount on the left of the equal sign has the same value as the amount on the right.

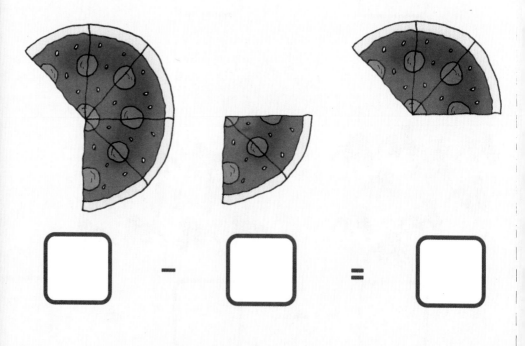

$$\boxed{} - \boxed{} = \boxed{}$$

Taking Flight

Count the birds sitting on the branches.

Count the birds that have flown away.

Subtract to find how many birds are left.

Subtraction

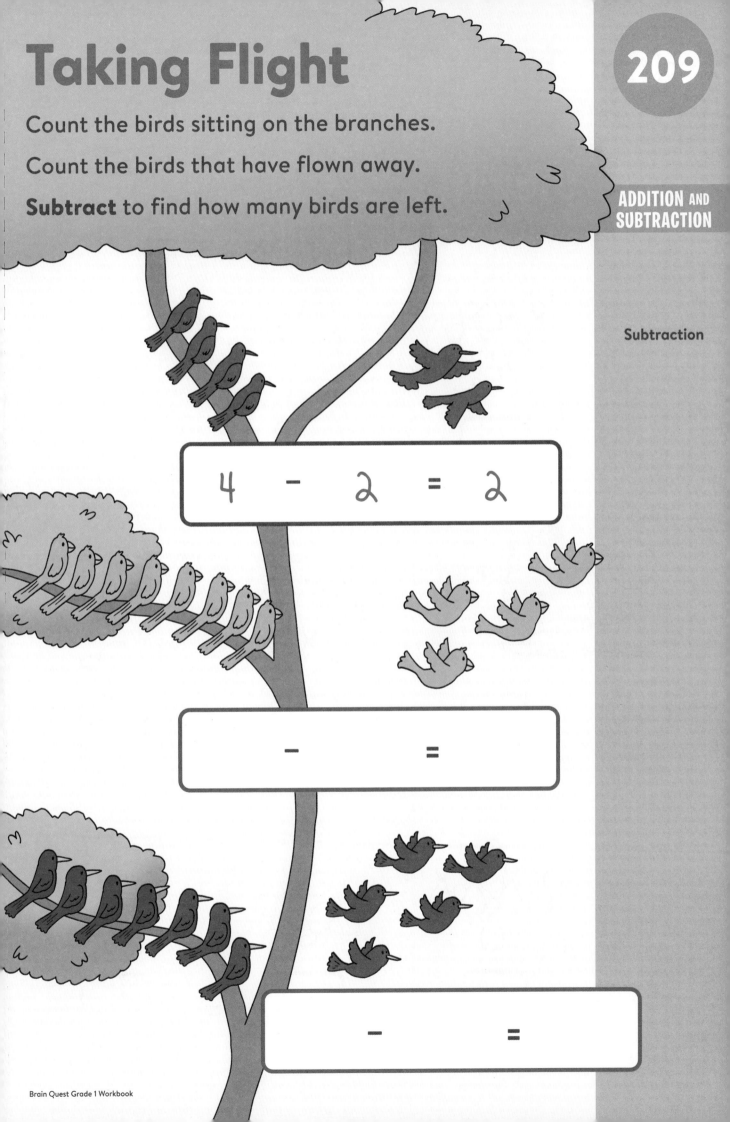

4   −   2   =   2

−   =

−   =

Let's Bowl!

Count how many pins are standing.

Count how many pins fall.

Subtract to tell how many pins are left.

Subtraction

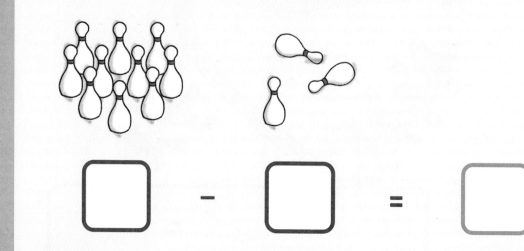

$$\boxed{} - \boxed{} = \boxed{}$$

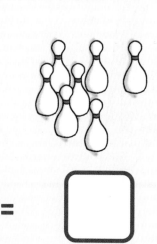 

$$\boxed{} = \boxed{} - \boxed{}$$

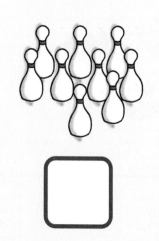 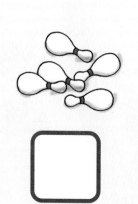

$$\boxed{} - \boxed{} = \boxed{}$$

Doggy Dessert

Count the dog bones.

Count how many bones the dog hides.

Subtract to tell how many bones are left.

Subtraction

Falling Leaves

Count the leaves in each group.

Write a subtraction sentence to find the **difference** between the two groups.

Subtraction

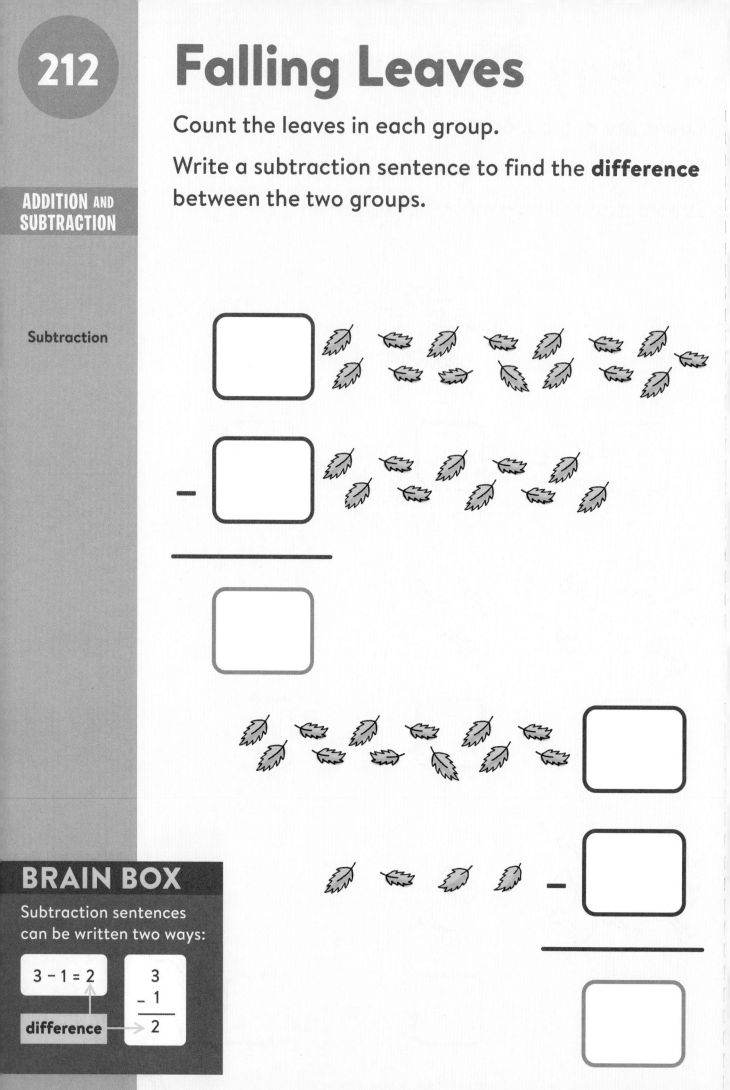

Sea Turtles

Count the sea turtles in each group.

Write a subtraction sentence to find the **difference** between the two groups.

Subtraction

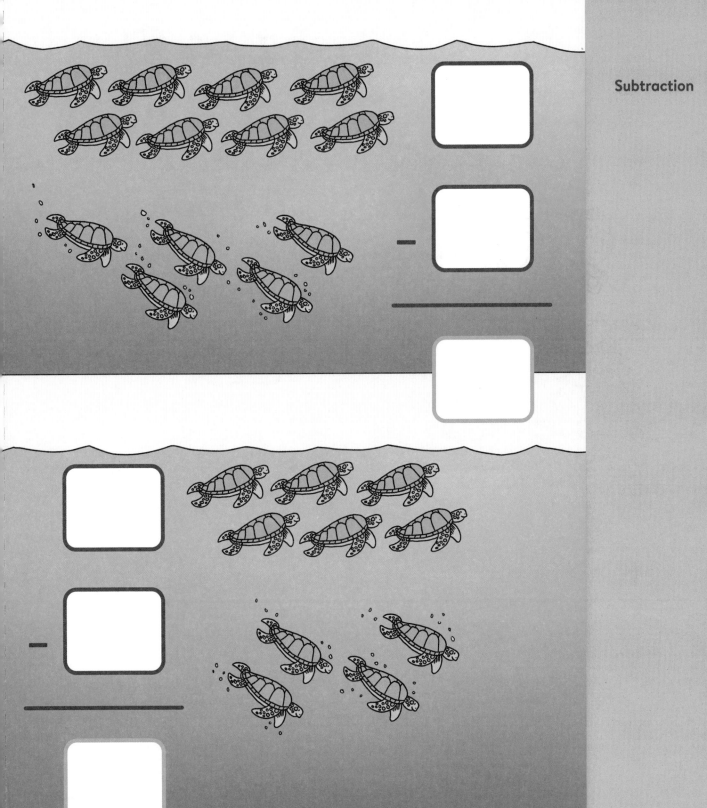

Go in the Snow!

Subtract the numbers.

Write the **difference** in the box.

Subtraction

7 – 5 = ☐

5 – 1 = ☐

☐ = 12 – 2

3 – 1 = ☐

8	6	7	7
– 4	– 3	– 4	– 3
☐	☐	☐	☐

7 − 1 = ☐

☐ = 5 − 2

5 − 3 = ☐

10 − 3 = ☐

☐ = 9 − 5

☐ = 7 − 6

8 − 2 = ☐

9 − 8 = ☐

4 − 2 = ☐

4 − 3 = ☐

$$\begin{array}{r} 2 \\ -\ 1 \\ \hline \end{array}$$
☐

$$\begin{array}{r} 4 \\ -\ 4 \\ \hline \end{array}$$
☐

$$\begin{array}{r} 8 \\ -\ 3 \\ \hline \end{array}$$
☐

$$\begin{array}{r} 10 \\ -\ 5 \\ \hline \end{array}$$
☐

The Magic Word

Add or **subtract** the numbers.

Write the answers in the boxes.

Addition and subtraction

O

7 + 13 = ☐

E

10 − 5 = ☐

P

8 − 7 = ☐

R

12 − 8 = ☐

6
+ 4
☐
S

20
− 5
☐
T

Figure out the wizard's magic word. Write the letters that match the numbers in the boxes.

| 1 | 4 | 5 | 10 | 15 | 20 |

☐ ☐ ☐ ☐ ☐ ☐

SHAPES AND MEASUREMENT

Look around. Can you spot an object shaped like a square? What about a circle? I like to search for shapes everywhere! Would you like to help me find shapes?

PARENTS In first grade, children learn to identify attributes of shapes and to quantify length and height using standard and nonstandard measurements. To strengthen their understanding of these concepts, practice finding and identifying shapes around your home or outdoors. You can also measure the shapes with a ruler or nonstandard tools like paper clips or your thumbs.

For additional resources, visit www.BrainQuest.com/grade1

Rocket Round-Up!

Can you find shapes in and around these rockets?

Color the triangles **blue**.

Color the stars **yellow**.

Color the ovals **red**.

Color the circles **orange**.

Color the squares **green**.

Color the diamonds **purple**.

Identifying
shapes

What Shape Is It?

Draw a line from the picture to the word that describes what shape it is.

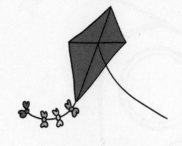

circle

square

oval

diamond

rectangle

triangle

Quiz Me!

Answer the questions about shapes.

How many sides does a square have?

How many corners does a diamond have?

How many sides does a triangle have?

How many corners does a circle have?

How many corners does a rectangle have?

BRAIN BOX

A **side** is the straight line between two corners of a shape. A **corner** is where two sides of a shape meet.

Shape Match

Draw a line from each card to the matching shape.

triangle

diamond

circle

rectangle

oval

square

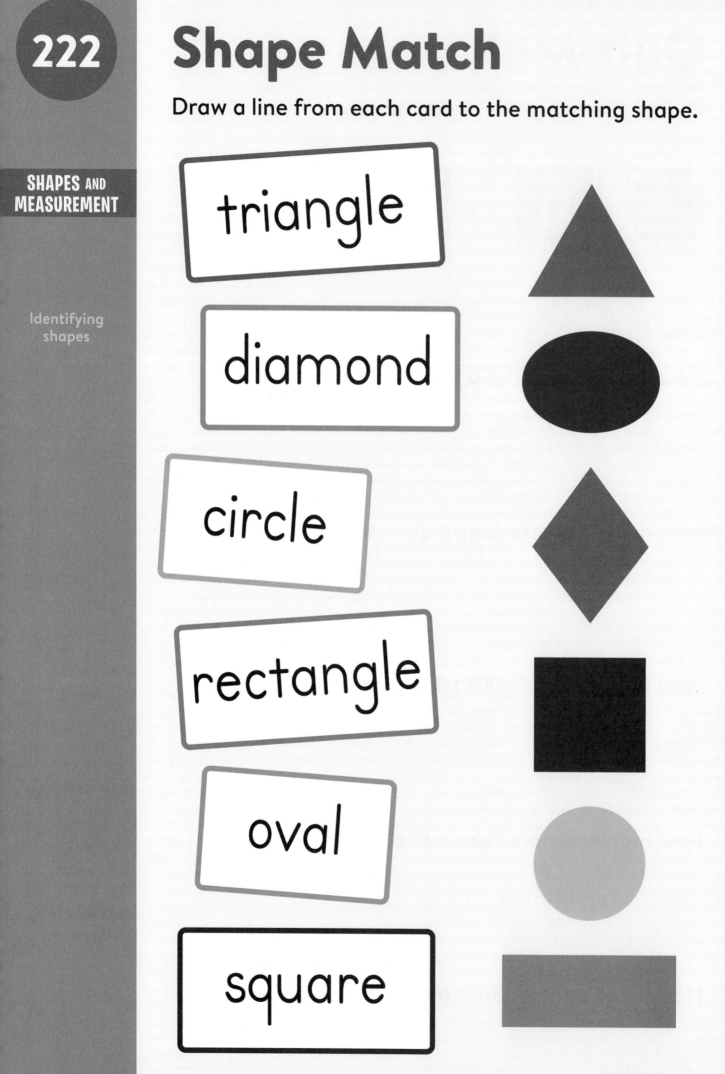

Connect the Dots!

Connect the dots to make each shape. Color each shape the same color as the dots.

Rulers Rule!

Look at the **ruler.** It is 6 inches long.

Measurements

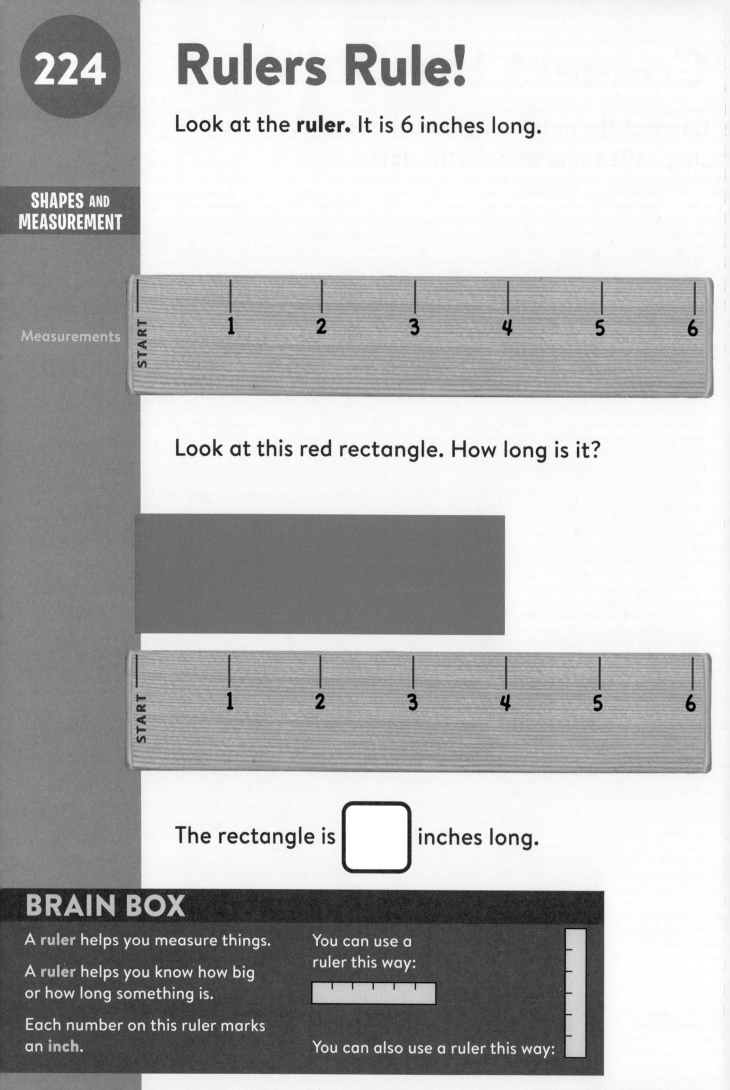

START 1 2 3 4 5 6

Look at this red rectangle. How long is it?

START 1 2 3 4 5 6

The rectangle is ⬜ inches long.

BRAIN BOX

A **ruler** helps you measure things.

A **ruler** helps you know how big or how long something is.

Each number on this ruler marks an **inch.**

You can use a ruler this way:

You can also use a ruler this way:

More Rulers!

How tall is this green rectangle?

The rectangle is ☐ inches tall.

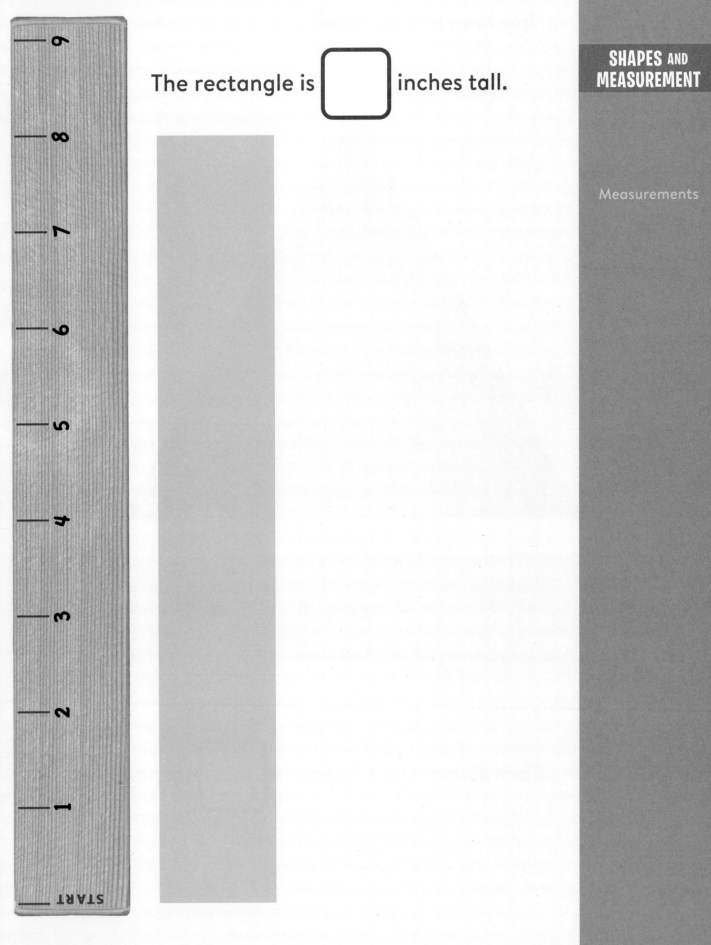

Measure the Triangle

The sides of this purple triangle are all the same.

How long is each side?

Measurements

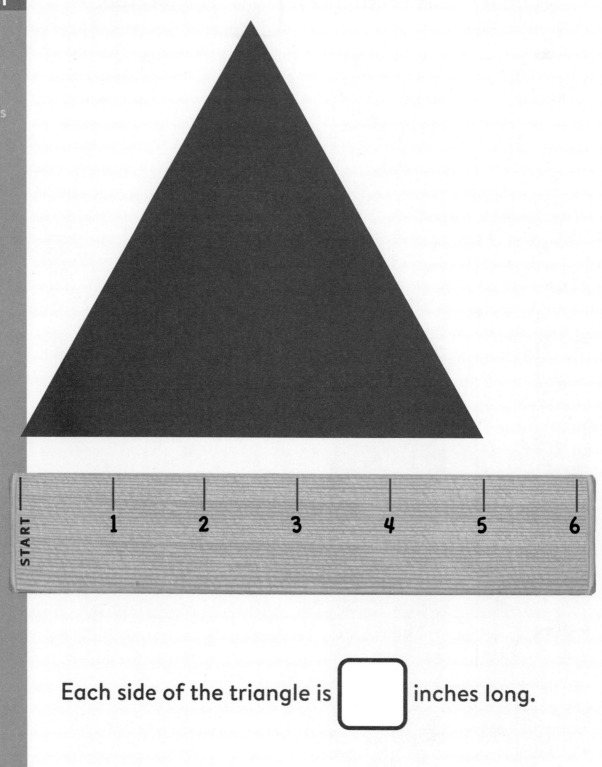

Each side of the triangle is [ ] inches long.

Comparing Shapes

Measuring can help you compare.

Circle the shape that is taller.

How tall is the blue square?  inches

How tall is the red rectangle? inches

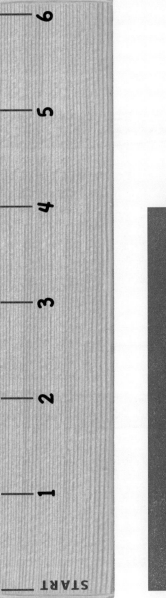

Sssssssnakes!

How long is each snake?

Write the number of inches next to each snake's head.

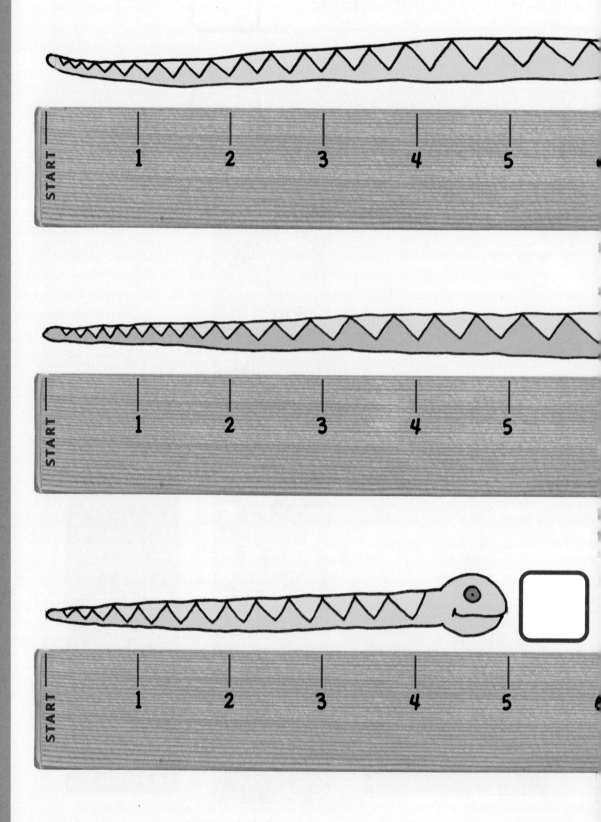

Which snake is the shortest?

Draw a circle around the shortest snake.

Measurements

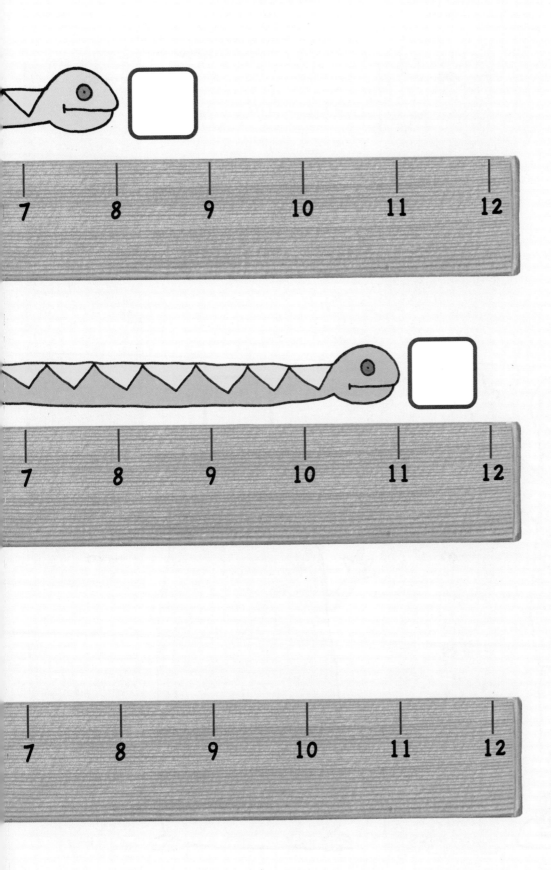

Monsters Measure!

How tall is each monster?

Write the number of inches above each monster.

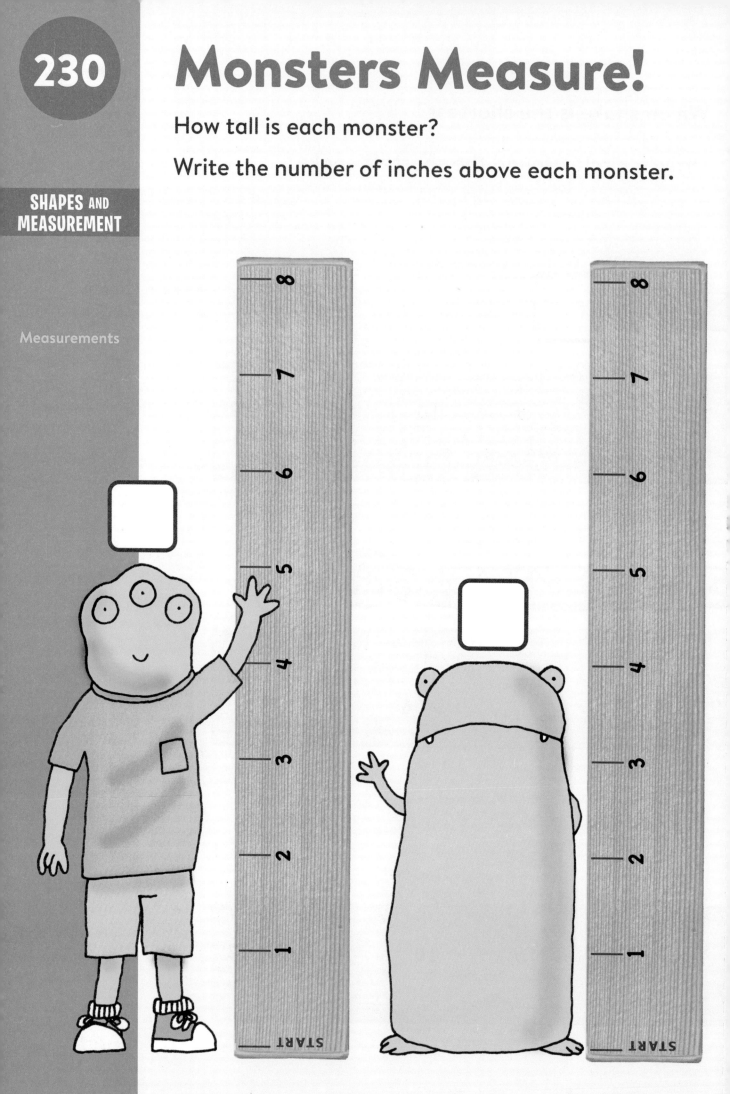

Which monster is tallest?

Circle the tallest monster.

Measurements

Lawn Bowling

How far did each kid roll the ball?

Write the number of inches above each ball.

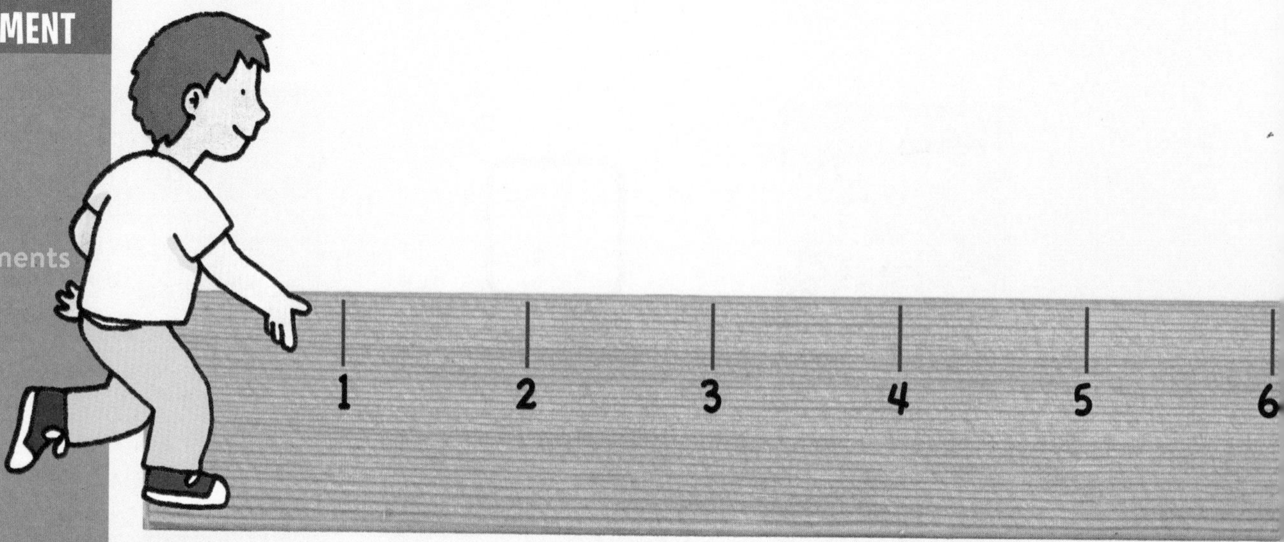

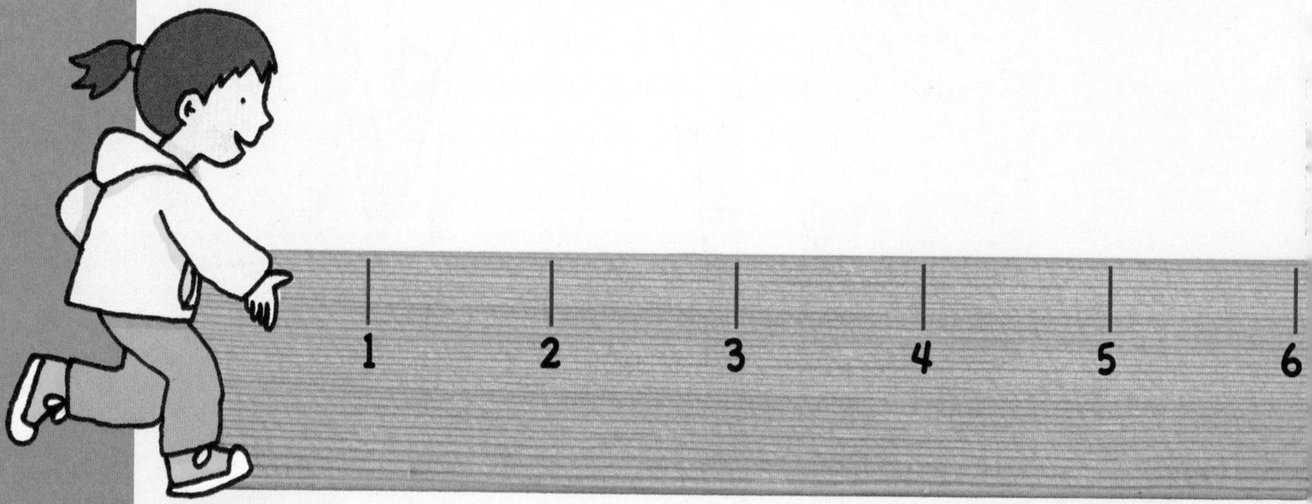

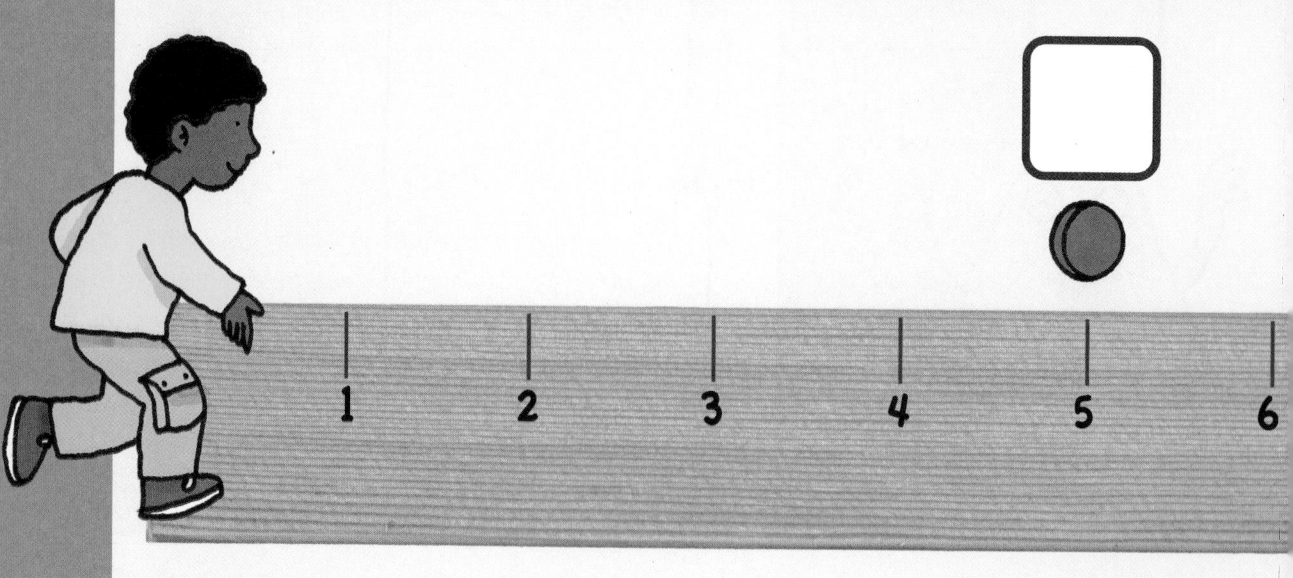

Measurements

1   2   3   4   5   6

1   2   3   4   5   6

1   2   3   4   5   6

Whose ball rolled the farthest?

Circle the ball that rolled the farthest.

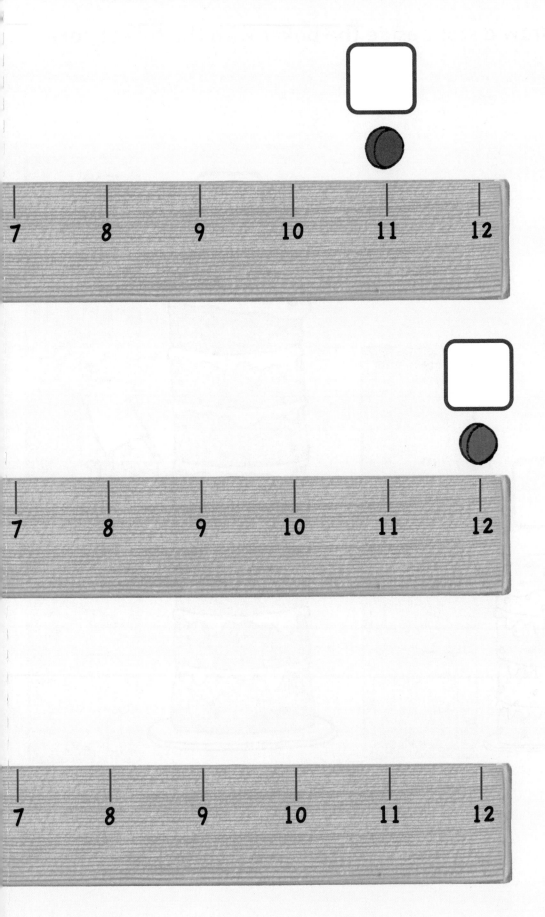

Cake Bake-Off

How tall is each cake?

Write the number of inches above each cake.

Draw a star beside the baker with the tallest cake.

Measurements

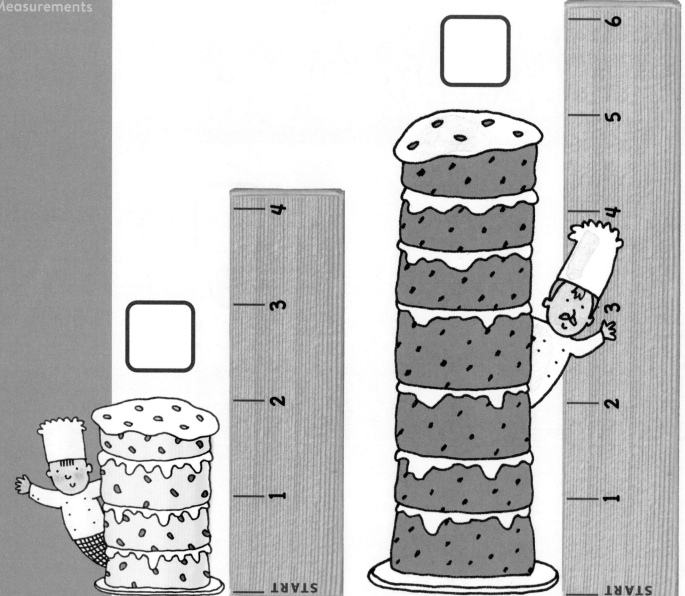

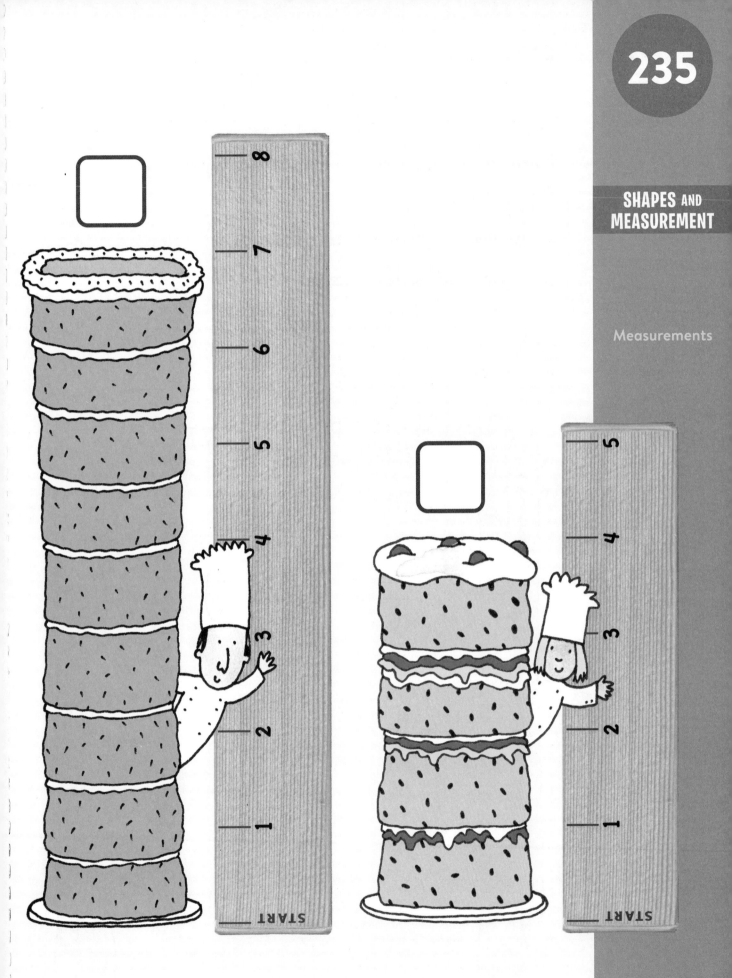

Shape Pictures

Look at the shapes.

Think of a picture you can draw with these shapes.

Draw your picture in the frame.

You can add other shapes too.

TIME AND MONEY

Joke time! What fish costs the most? A . . . goldfish! Are you ready to have fun with time and money? Let's get ready to tell time and count coins!

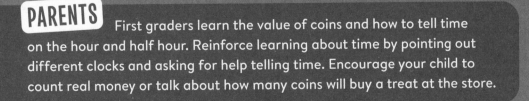

PLACE A STICKER HERE

Broken Clock!

Can you help fix the **clock**?

Write the missing numbers in the circles.

Telling time

12

10

2

8

4

5

BRAIN BOX

A **clock** has 12 numbers. Each number stands for one hour.

A clock has a **little hand**. It points to the hour.

A clock has a **big hand**. It points to the minutes.

Clock Shop

What time is it?

Write the time on the line below each clock.

3:00

_____

_____   _____

_____   _____

The **little
hand** is
pointing to
the **3**.

The **big hand**
is pointing to
the **12**.

That means
it's **3:00**.

Catch the Train!

Read the times on the train schedule.

Draw a line to the watch with that time.

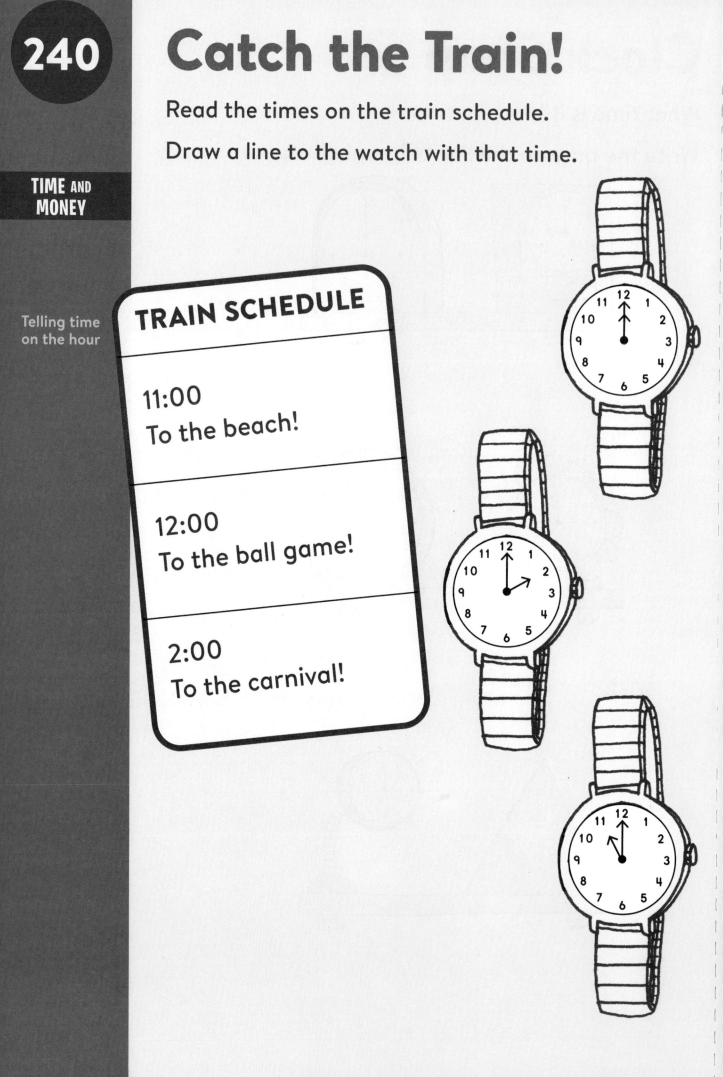

TRAIN SCHEDULE

11:00
To the beach!

12:00
To the ball game!

2:00
To the carnival!

TRAIN SCHEDULE

3:00
To the horse show!

4:00
To the pizza party!

7:00
To the mountains!

Beach	11:00
Basketball	12:00
Carnival	2:00
Horse show	3:00
Pizza Party	4:00
Mountains	7:00

Show the Half Hour

Write the time below each clock.

12:30

BRAIN BOX

Look at
this clock:

The little hand is pointing between the
3 and the **4**. The big hand is pointing
to the **6**. When the big hand points
to the **6**, it shows the half hour. This
clock says that it is **3:30**.

Matching clocks

Two Kinds of Clocks

Draw a line to match the clocks that show the same time.

Ticktock!

Draw the hands on the clock to show the time written below.

1:30

7:30

9:30

3:00

6:00

12:30

Coin value

Pennies, Nickels, Dimes

How many pennies make a nickel?

Count the pennies. Write the number.

pennies =

How many pennies make a dime?

Count the pennies. Write the number.

pennies =

How many nickels make a dime?

Count the nickels. Write the number.

nickels =

Total Cents

Write the number of ¢ in the box below each coin.

Then add the money.

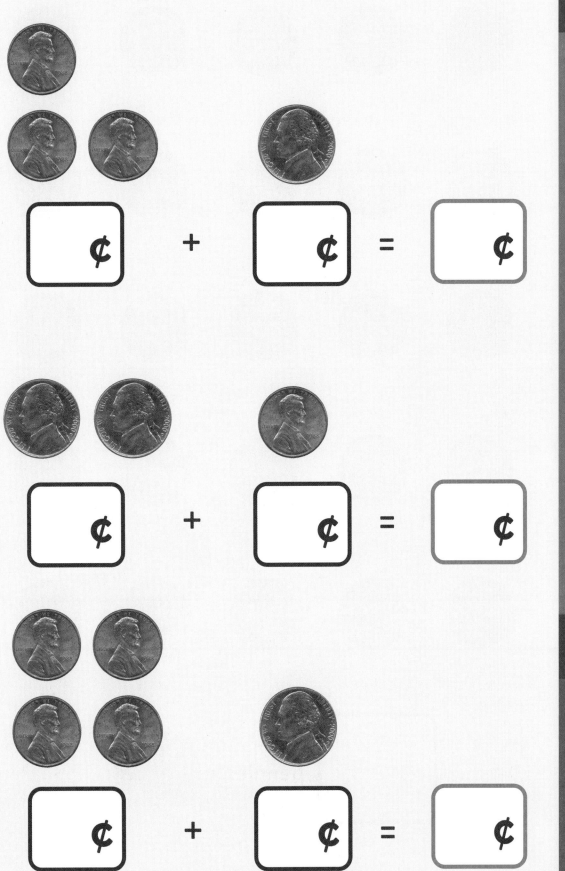

BRAIN BOX

The symbol ¢ means **cents**.

A penny is worth 1 cent.

You can write 1 cent like this: 1¢.

Coin value

Quarters

How many pennies make a quarter?

Count the pennies. Write the number.

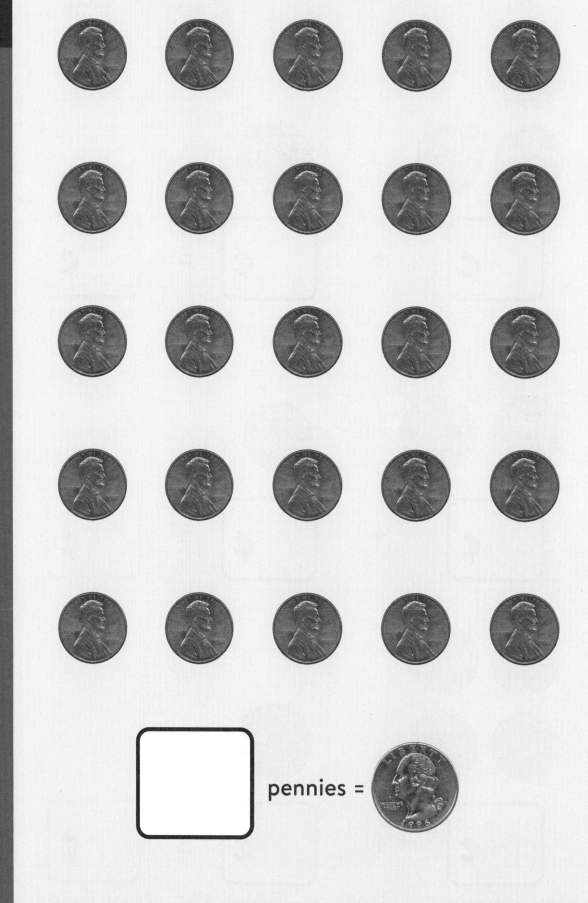

☐ pennies =

How else can you make a quarter?
Add the coins to find out!

Coin value

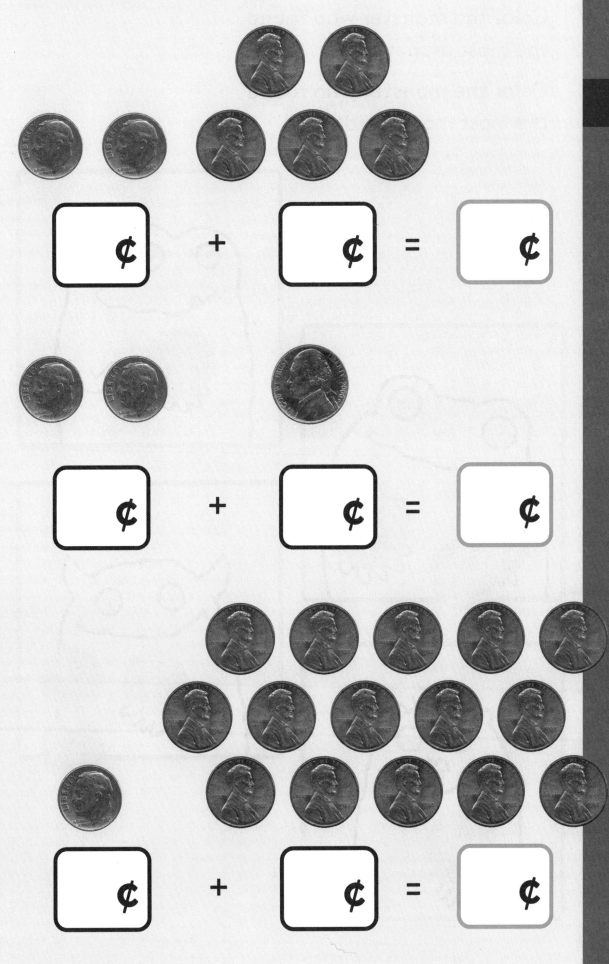

$$\boxed{}\text{¢} \quad + \quad \boxed{}\text{¢} \quad = \quad \boxed{}\text{¢}$$

$$\boxed{}\text{¢} \quad + \quad \boxed{}\text{¢} \quad = \quad \boxed{}\text{¢}$$

$$\boxed{}\text{¢} \quad + \quad \boxed{}\text{¢} \quad = \quad \boxed{}\text{¢}$$

Lucky Monsters!

Color the monster who found
the most money **green**.

Color the monster who found
the least money **red**.

Identifying
money

Which Is More?

Write the money value.

Circle the money that is worth the most.

¢

¢

¢

¢

¢

¢

¢

¢

Pick the Right Price

Read the price on each vase.

Draw a line to the group of coins you need to buy it.

Comparing
money value

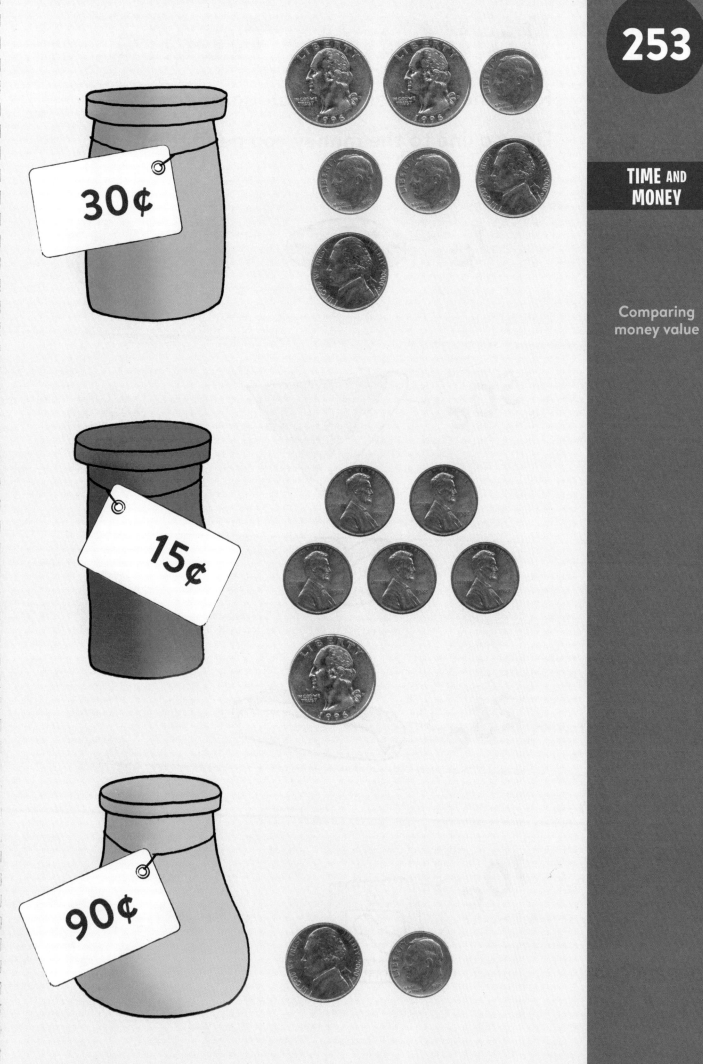

30¢

15¢

90¢

Ball-Game Treats

Read the price for each ball-game treat.

Draw a line to the money you need to buy it.

SOCIAL STUDIES

Let's talk about where we live. What stores are near you? Who are the helpers in your neighborhood? Are you ready to learn about all the people and places that help make up a community?

PARENTS Children can better understand how people live and work in communities by thinking about the goods and services we use and the people who provide them. Talk about your community. Name people your child knows who help your community thrive.

PLACE A STICKER HERE

For additional resources, visit www.BrainQuest.com/grade1

Home Sweet Home

Complete the sentences to tell about where you live.

The name of my street is

.

The name of my city or town is

.

The name of my state is

.

Your Community

Think about your neighborhood.

Draw your favorite place to go.

Community
awareness

Write a sentence about why you like this place.

We Need Farms!

Most foods we eat and things we drink come from farms.

Circle the things we get from farms.

From the Farm

The plants on the left were grown on farms.

Draw a line to match each plant to the food we get from it.

Goods to Buy

People make the goods we buy.

Draw a line to match the person with the thing they made.

Goods and services

On Our Way!

How should these kids get to the playground? Draw a line on the map to show them the most direct path.

Help these friends find the animal shelter.
Draw a line on the map to show them the most
direct path.

Let's Go on a Walk

Show this family how to get around the park.

Draw a red line on the path to the lake.

Draw a blue line on the path to the picnic tables.

Maps

VISITORS' CENTER

ENTER

Draw a green line on the path to the butterfly garden.

Draw an orange line on the path to the visitors' center.

Maps

BUTTERFLY GARDEN

It's a Sign!

The letters on these signs are all mixed up!

Unscramble the letters on each sign and write the correct word below.

SCIENCE

Are you curious? Do you like to ask questions? Let's think like scientists and find out about Earth, the sun, the seasons, and more.

PARENTS Talking about seasons and tracking the weather are tangible and relatable ways to introduce science. Young learners are natural scientists. They ask a lot of questions and make observations about how the world works. By encouraging their curiosity and exploration, you can help your child develop a love of science.

PLACE A STICKER HERE

Our Earth

Read about Earth.

On the globe below, color all the land parts brown. Color all the water parts blue.

Earth is the planet we live on.

It has land and water.

The Sun

Read about the sun.

Write the answers to the questions on the lines below.

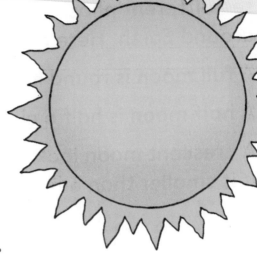

The sun is a star.

The sun is very important.

It gives us light.

It gives us heat.

Without the sun, we could not survive.

Earth travels around the sun once per year.

This is called an orbit.

Is the sun a moon or a star?

What does the sun give us?

The Moon

Read about the moon.

The moon reflects light from the sun. We see different phases of the moon as it travels around Earth. Here are some moon phases:

A full moon is round like a circle.

A half moon is half a circle.

A crescent moon looks like a sideways smile. It is smaller than a half moon.

Label the phases of the moon.

What kind of moon do you see tonight?

Light

Read about light.

Is light white? No! Light is made up of colors. When light passes through raindrops, high above Earth, the light rays bend. When light bends, we see the colors of the rainbow.

R for **red**
O for **orange**
Y for yellow
G for **green**
B for **blue**
I for **indigo**
V for **violet**

Color the rainbow.

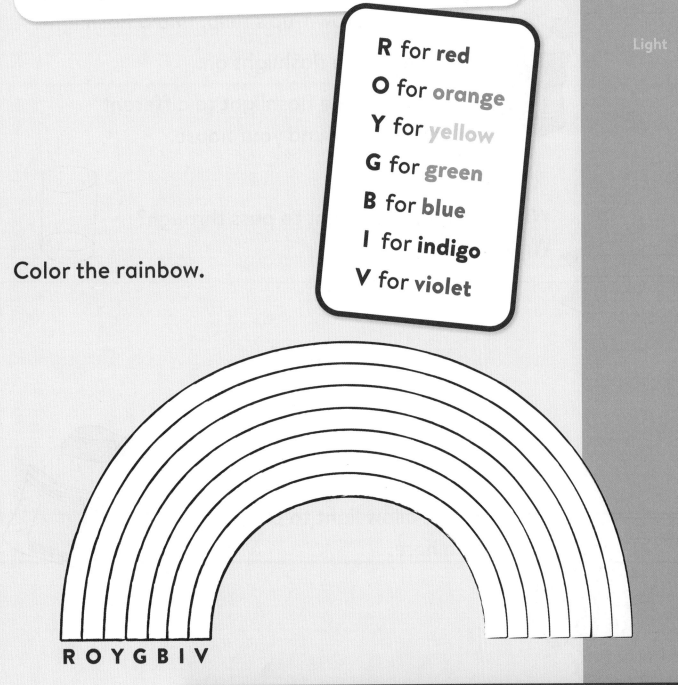

ROYGBIV

BRAIN BOX

What are the colors of the **rainbow**? You can remember the colors of the rainbow in order by remembering the name "ROY G. BIV."

Light Experiment

Light can pass through some objects but not others.

Objects that are **transparent** allow light to pass through.

Objects that are **opaque** do not allow light to pass through.

With a grown-up's help, find a flashlight.

Switch the flashlight on.

Hold up the flashlight to different objects around your house.

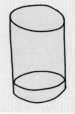

Which objects allow light to pass through?
Write them here.

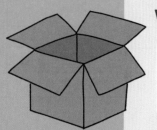

Which do not allow light to pass through?
Write them here.

Sound Experiment

Sounds are made by **vibrations**.

Vibrations happen when objects move back and forth.

We can use everyday objects like rubber bands to learn about vibrations.

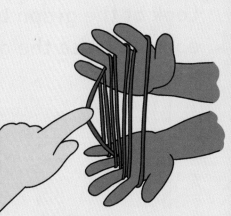

With a grown-up's help, find some rubber bands.

Stretch them between your fingers.

Ask a grown-up or friend to pluck them.

Can you feel them move or vibrate?

How do they sound if they are loose?

How do they sound if they are stretched tight?

274

Snowy Week

It snowed a lot this week!

Look at the graph to see how much it snowed each day. Use the graph to answer the questions.

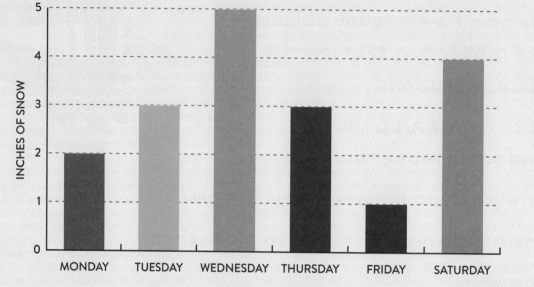

On which day did it snow the most?

On which day did it snow the least?

On which two days did it snow the same amount?

What's the Weather?

Keep a weather log for one week.

Describe the weather. Was it sunny? Windy? Rainy?

Monday

Tuesday

Wednesday

Thursday

Friday

Saturday

Sunday

Butterfly Life Cycle

Read about the butterfly's life cycle.

Then label each stage of the life cycle on the picture.

Butterflies are insects that go through this life cycle:

First, a butterfly lays an egg.

The egg hatches into a caterpillar.

After eating a lot, the caterpillar spins a chrysalis.

Inside the chrysalis, the caterpillar turns into an adult.

Soon, the adult emerges, or comes out, from the chrysalis.

A new butterfly is born!

A Person's Life Cycle

Draw yourself as a baby.

Draw yourself now.

Draw yourself as
a grown-up!

Solids and Liquids

Read about solids and liquids.

Write the letter **S** below the solid things.

Write the letter **L** below the liquid things.

Some things do not change their shape.

They are **solids**.

Some things are **liquid**.

Liquids can change shape.

S

It's Good to Recycle!

Read about recycling.

Circle the things at this party that can be recycled.

> We can turn old things into new things.
> This is called recycling.
> We can recycle cans.
> We can recycle paper.
> We can recycle bottles.

Drop It in the Bin

Look at the picture on each bin.

Draw a line from all the things you can recycle to the correct bin.

PLASTIC

PAPER

CANS

TECHNOLOGY

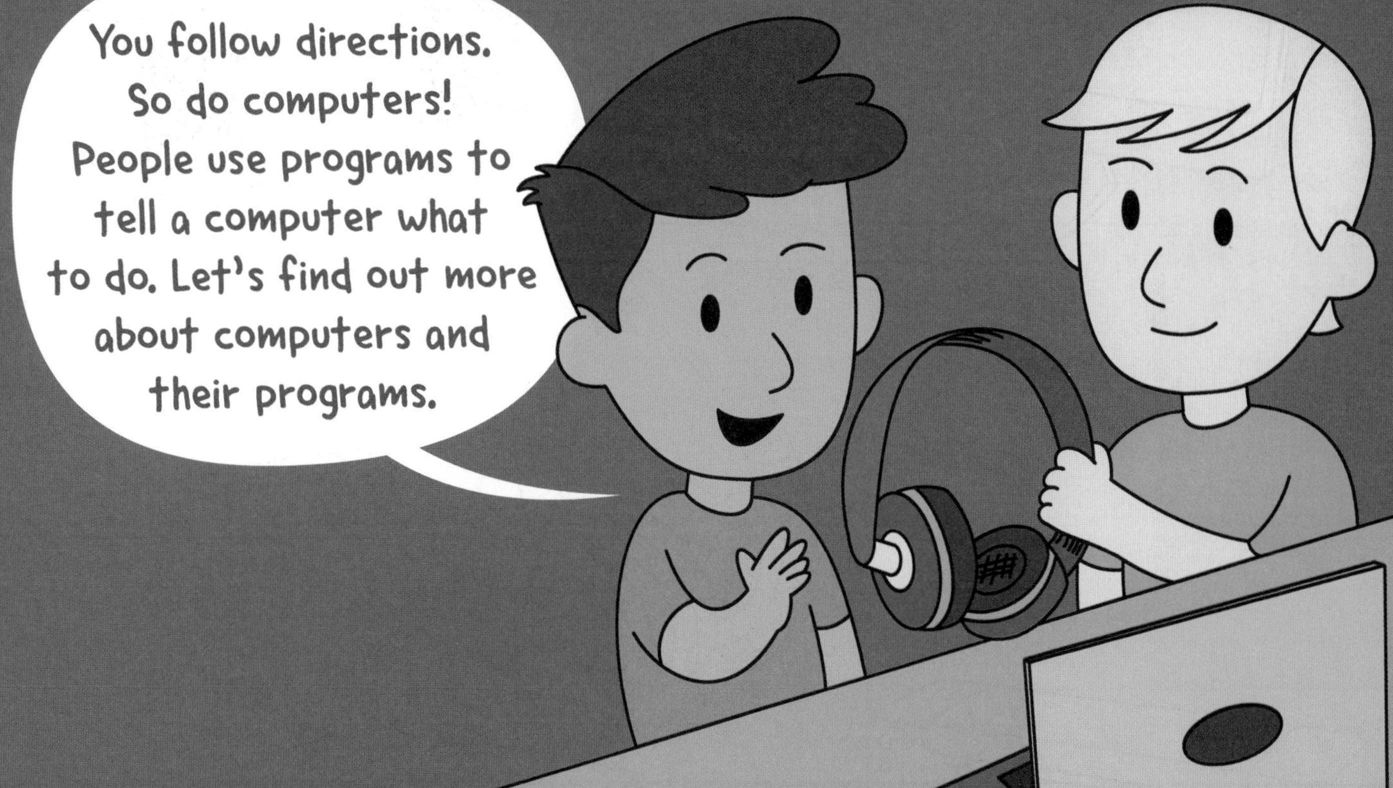

You follow directions. So do computers! People use programs to tell a computer what to do. Let's find out more about computers and their programs.

PARENTS Help your child build a foundation in computer science by familiarizing them with the names for the different parts of a computer. Point out their interactions with computers and technology, like playing games on tablets, taking photos with cell phones, or using a remote control.

PLACE A STICKER HERE

For additional resources, visit www.BrainQuest.com/grade1

Hardware Hunt

Color the hardware that plays sound **blue**.

Color the hardware we use to type words **red**.

Color the hardware we use to print **yellow**.

Color the hardware that shows or displays pictures and words **purple**.

Hardware

BRAIN BOX

Hardware is any part of a computer that we can see or touch. Different kinds of hardware have different jobs. For example, some hardware plays sound—you can listen to music with a speaker or headphones.

Home Row

We use the **keyboard** to type on a computer.
We can use a keyboard to type directions:

GO BACK 3.

Keyboard

Find the keys you need to type the directions. Make
the keys the same color as the letters.

Find the space key. Color it **pink**.

Directions
and code

Out of Order!

These steps are not in sequence, which means they are out of order. Can you put them in order?

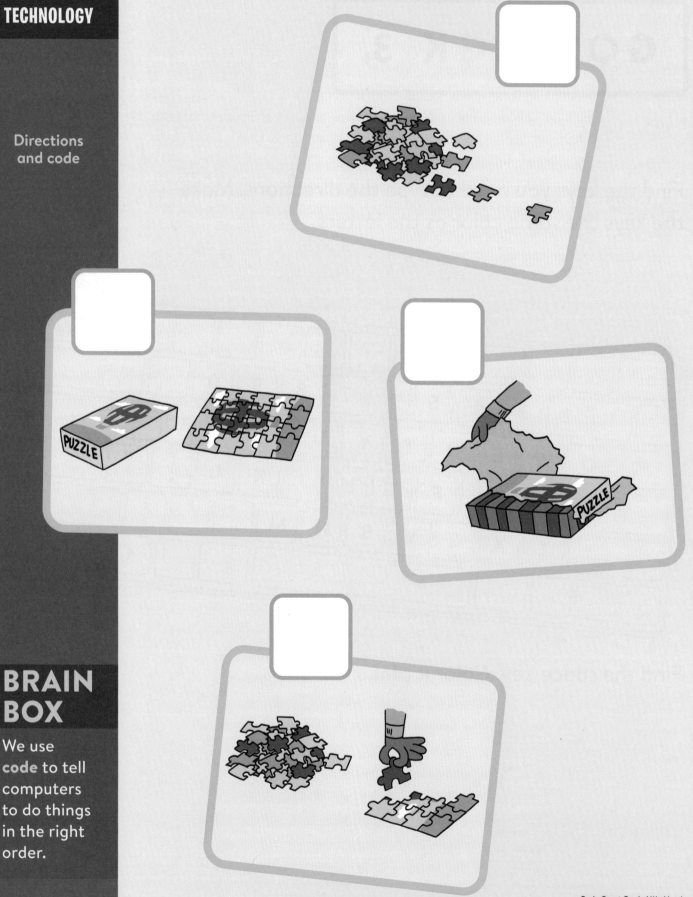

BRAIN BOX

We use **code** to tell computers to do things in the right order.

Race Car

Draw arrows to move the race car to the finish line.

Sequencing and code

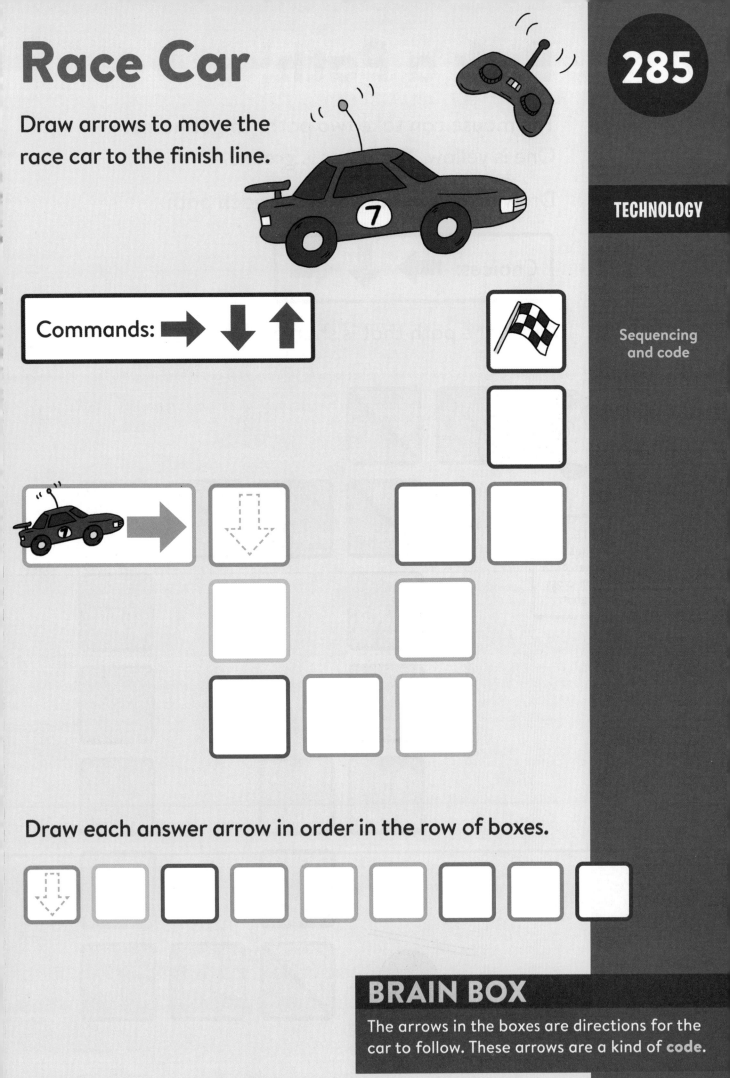

Commands: ➡ ⬇ ⬆

Draw each answer arrow in order in the row of boxes.

BRAIN BOX

The arrows in the boxes are directions for the car to follow. These arrows are a kind of **code**.

Pick a Path!

The mouse can take two paths to get home.
One is yellow. The other is green.

Draw arrows in the boxes for each path.

Choices: ➡️ ⬇️ ⬅️

Circle the path that is shorter.

NOTE:
If a box has two colors, then both paths can cross through it.

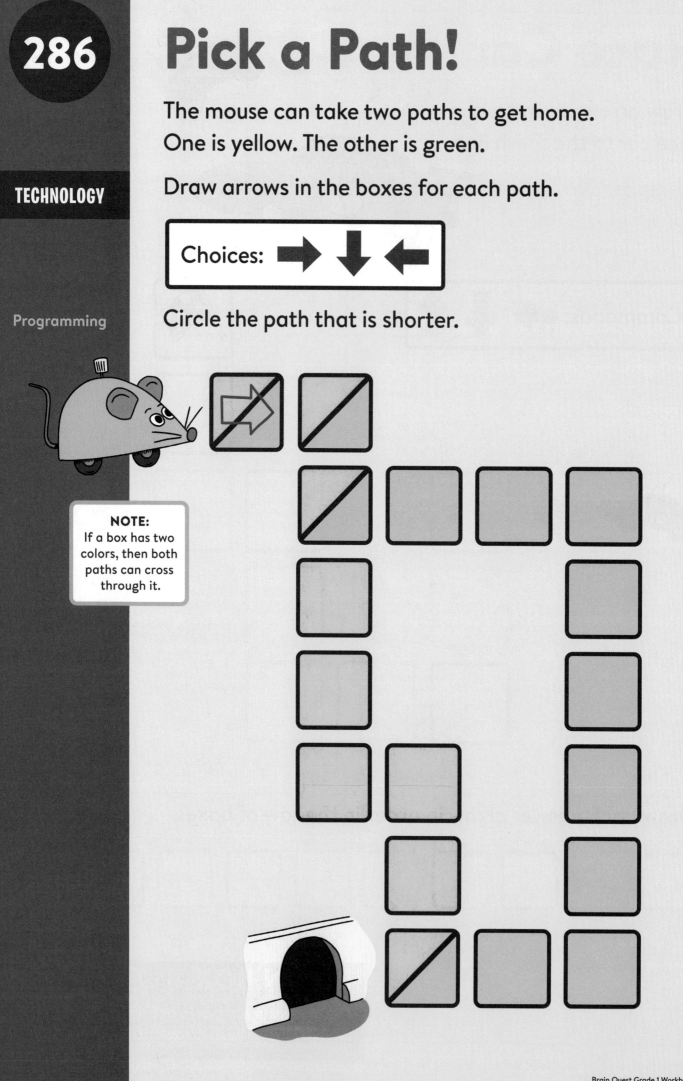

New Battery

Help the robot reach the battery.

In order, draw each arrow you see in the box below into each box of the path.

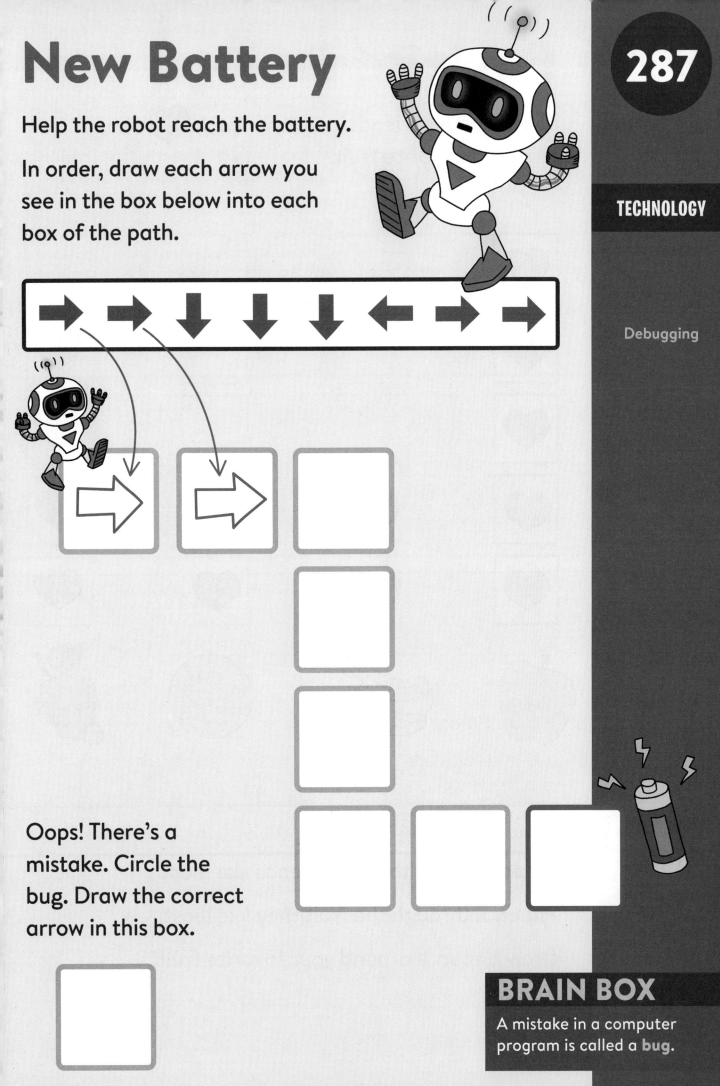

Oops! There's a mistake. Circle the bug. Draw the correct arrow in this box.

BRAIN BOX

A mistake in a computer program is called a **bug**.

Favorite Fruit

Jamal and his friends love fruit. Each  shows a friend's favorite fruit.

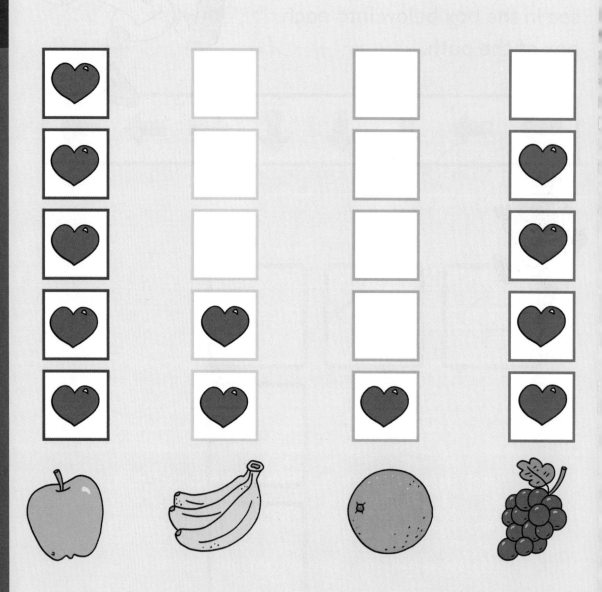

Circle the fruit that the friends like most.

Put an **X** through the fruit they like least.

Draw a square around your favorite fruit!

Fall Leaves

Color the leaves. Count each kind.

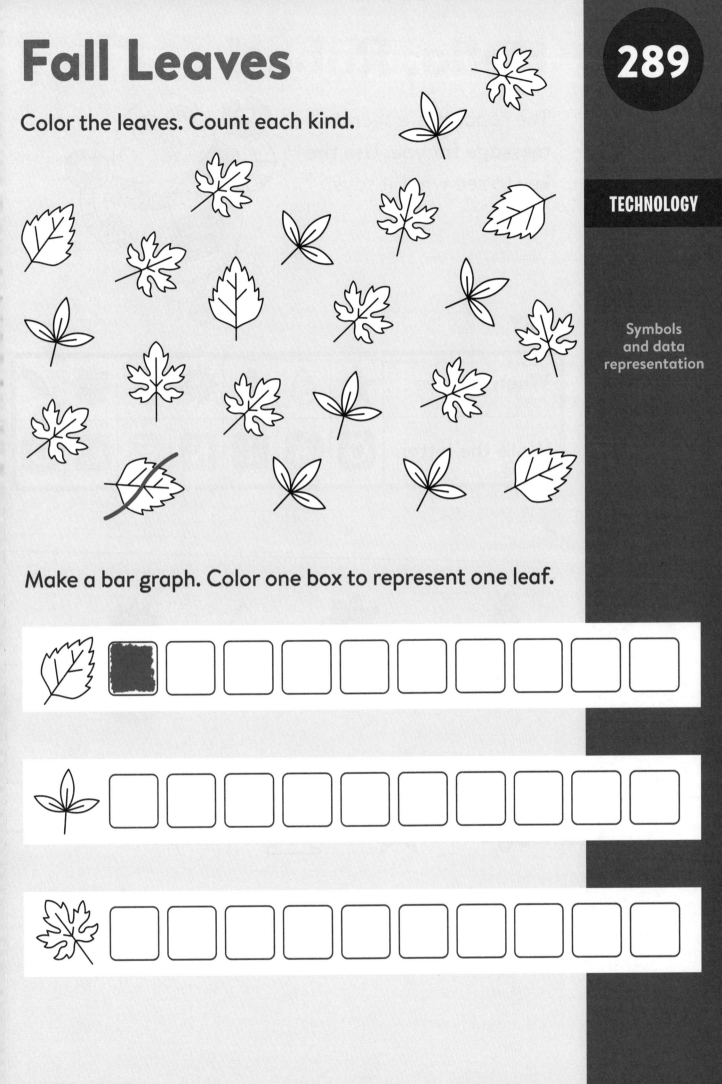

Make a bar graph. Color one box to represent one leaf.

Hello, Robot!

The robot has a secret message for you. Use the key to see what it says!

KEY

When you see . . .	★	💧	🌲	☀	❄	🌼	🌈
Write the letter	O	A	I	N	E	C	D

 🌲   🌼   💧   ☀

☐   ☐   ☐   ☐

 🌼   ★   🌈   ❄

☐   ☐   ☐   ☐ !

ANSWER KEY

Some problems have only one answer. Some problems have many answers. Turn the page to check your work.

BRAIN QUEST 1 WORKBOOK

For additional resources, visit www.BrainQuest.com/grade1

Super Safari! (pages 8–9)

The names of these animals all start with the b, d, or f sound. Say the word for each animal. What beginning sound do you hear? Write the letter.

dog fly bat
deer frog bear
fox duck beaver

BRAIN BOX A consonant is any letter in the alphabet that is not a vowel.

To the Castle! (pages 10–11)

The things in this picture all start with the h, j, k, or q sound. Say the word for each picture. What beginning sound do you hear? Write the letter.

quilt
harp hat queen king
jar
kitten jester

Monster Manor! (pages 12–13)

The things in this picture all start with the l, m, n, or p sound. Say the word for each picture. What beginning sound do you hear? Write the letter.

monkey moon
net
puzzle lollipop
monster noodles
lizard pizza

Blast Off! (pages 14–15)

The things in this picture all start with the r, s, or t sound. Say the word for each picture. What beginning sound do you hear? Write the letter.

raccoon
seal turtle tiger
rocket rabbit
snake telescope

Wacky Wizard! (pages 16–17)

The things in this picture all start with the v, w, x, y, or z sound. Say the word for each picture. What beginning sound do you hear? Write the letter.

wizard
vase
yo-yo zebra
whistle zipper yarn
vacuum x-ray

City and Country / Girl and Giant (pages 18–19)

Say the word for each picture. If you hear a hard c sound, draw a line to the country. If you hear a soft c sound, draw a line to the city.

country city

Say the word for each picture. If you hear a hard g sound, draw a line to the girl. If you hear a soft g sound, draw a line to the giant.

girl giant

BRAIN BOX

Web and Kid / Fun in the Sun (pages 20–21)

The words for these pictures all end in b or d. Say the word for each picture. What ending sound do you hear? Write the letter.

bird bread
crib kid
crab sled
web bib

The words for these pictures all end in m or n. Say the word for each picture. What ending sound do you hear? Write the letter.

sun
palm
swim
fan plum
clam
pen

Ship and Boat / Snail and Bus (pages 22–23)

The words for these pictures all end in p or t. Say the word for each picture. What ending sound do you hear? Write the letter.

ship boat
net boot
map peanut
pot sheep

The words for these pictures all end in l or ll, s or ss. Say the word for each picture. What ending sound do you hear? Write the letter.

snail bus
ball glass
doll dress
shell plus

Frog and Duck

The words for these pictures all end in **g** or **k**.
Say the word for each picture.
Circle the pictures that end with a **g** sound.
Underline the pictures that end with a **k** sound.

Chicken Checkers!

Say the word for each picture.
Circle the pictures that begin with the **ch** sound.

BRAIN BOX
Sometimes two consonants that are next to each other make a new sound.
Example: chip
When you say chip, you don't hear the c and h sounds separately. You hear the new ch sound.

Show Me!

Say the word for each picture.
Circle the pictures that begin with the **sh** sound.

BRAIN BOX
Sometimes two consonants that are next to each other make a new sound.
Example: shovel
When you say shovel, you don't hear the s and h sounds separately. You hear the new sh sound.

The Theater!

Say the word for each picture.
Circle the pictures that begin with the **th** sound.

BRAIN BOX
Sometimes two consonants that are next to each other make a new sound.
Example: theater
When you say theater, you don't hear the t and h sounds separately. You hear the new th sound.

Short a

Say the word for each picture.
Color the cards with pictures that have the **short a** sound.

BRAIN BOX
The letter a is a vowel. It can have two sounds: a short a sound, as in cat, or a long a sound, as in cane.

Short e

Say the word for each picture.
Color the cards with pictures that have the **short e** sound.

BRAIN BOX
The letter e is a vowel. It can have two sounds: a short e sound, as in bed, or a long e sound, as in bee.

Short i

Say the word for each picture.
Color the cards with pictures that have the **short i** sound.

BRAIN BOX
The letter i is a vowel. It can have two sounds: a short i sound, as in fish, or a long i sound, as in bike.

Short o

Say the word for each picture.
Color the cards with pictures that have the **short o** sound.

BRAIN BOX
The letter o is a vowel. It can have two sounds: a short o sound, as in pot, or a long o sound, as in go-go.

32

Short u

Say the word for each picture.
Color the cards with pictures that have the **short u** sound.

BRAIN BOX
The letter u is a vowel. It can have two sounds: a short u sound, as in sun, or a long u sound, as in cube.

Long a

Say the word for each picture.
Color the cards with pictures that have the **long a** sound.

BRAIN BOX
The letter a is a vowel. It can have two sounds: a short a sound, as in cat, or a long a sound, as in cane.

Long e

Say the word for each picture.
Color the cards with pictures that have the **long e** sound.

BRAIN BOX
The letter e is a vowel. It can have two sounds: a short e sound, as in bed, or a long e sound, as in Bee.

Long i

Say the word for each picture.
Color the cards with pictures that have the **long i** sound.

BRAIN BOX
The letter i is a vowel. It can have two sounds: a short i sound, as in fish, or a long i sound, as in bike.

Long o

Say the word for each picture.
Color the cards with pictures that have the **long o** sound.

BRAIN BOX
The letter o is a vowel. It can have two sounds: a short o sound, as in pot, or a long o sound, as in yo-yo.

Long u

Say the word for each picture.
Color the cards with pictures that have the **long u** sound.

BRAIN BOX
The letter u is a vowel. It can have two sounds: a short u sound, as in sun, or a long u sound, as in cube.

Long Vowel Review

Circle the word that has the same long vowel sound as the first word in that row.

toe	ox	(hope)	read
hike	cube	big	time
rain	lake	seem	bat
bee	pen	look	heel
huge	but	cube	flea

Jam and Cake

Say the word for each picture.
Draw a line from the pictures with the **short a** sound to the **jam**.
Draw a line from the pictures with the **long a** sound to the **cake**.

jam   cake

BRAIN BOX
The vowel a has two sounds: a short a sound, as in jam, or a long a sound, as in cake.

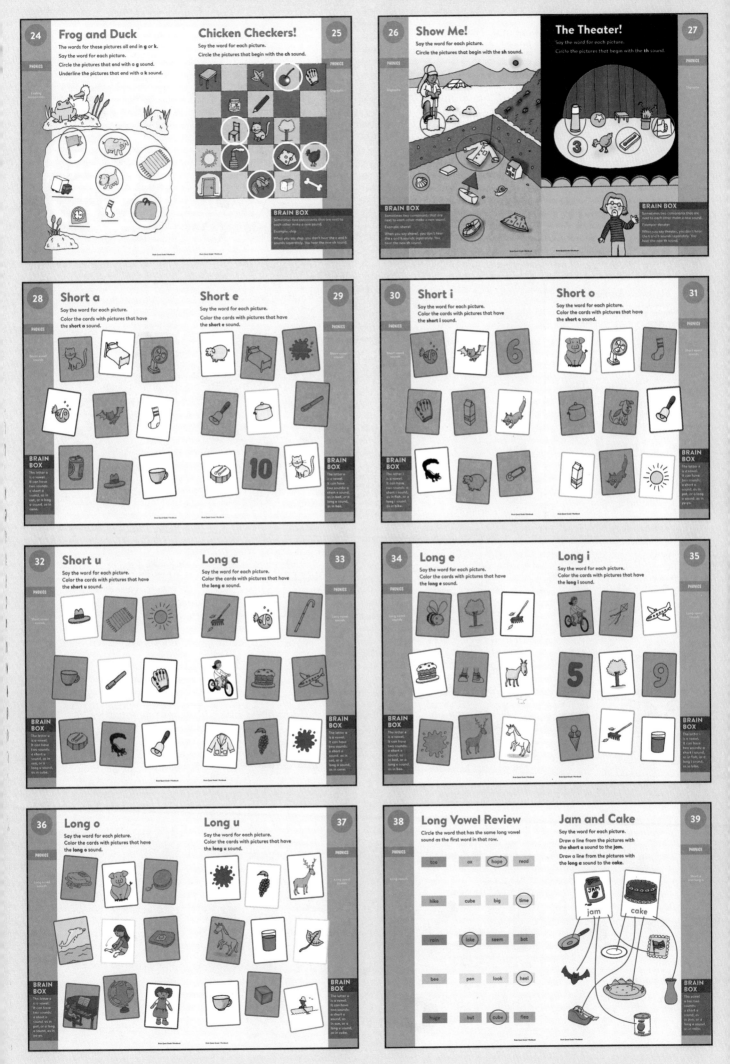

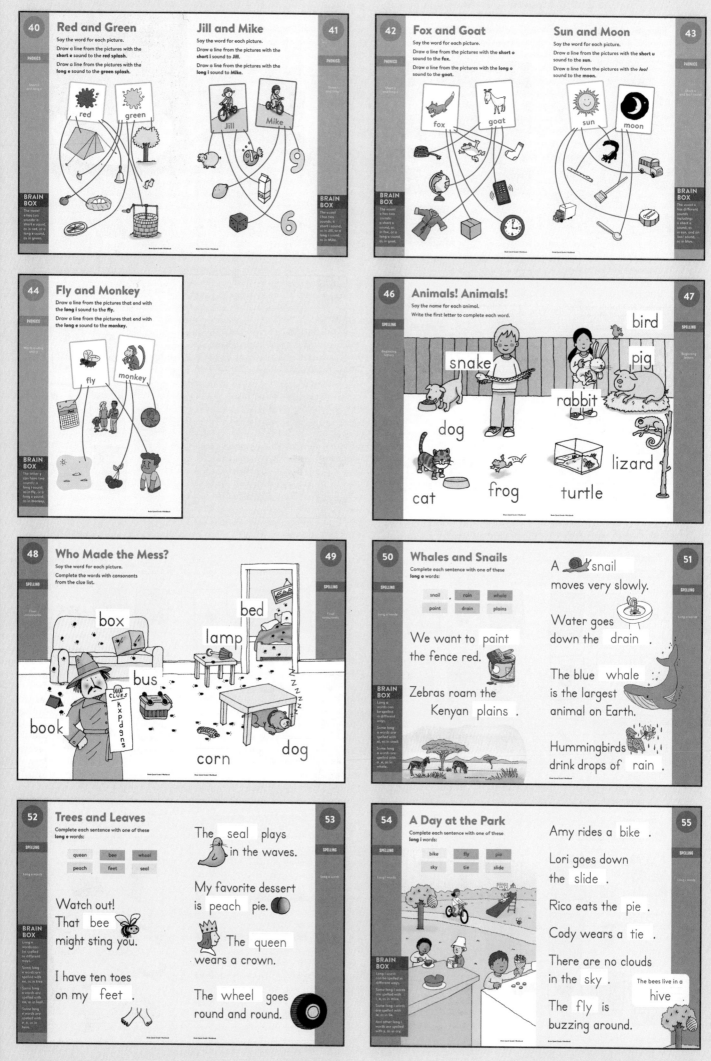

40 — Red and Green
Say the word for each picture.
Draw a line from the pictures with the **short e** sound to the **red splash**.
Draw a line from the pictures with the **long e** sound to the **green splash**.

red   green

41 — Jill and Mike
Say the word for each picture.
Draw a line from the pictures with the **short i** sound to **Jill**.
Draw a line from the pictures with the **long i** sound to **Mike**.

Jill   Mike

42 — Fox and Goat
Say the word for each picture.
Draw a line from the pictures with the **short o** sound to the **fox**.
Draw a line from the pictures with the **long o** sound to the **goat**.

fox   goat

43 — Sun and Moon
Say the word for each picture.
Draw a line from the pictures with the **short u** sound to the **sun**.
Draw a line from the pictures with the **/oo/** sound to the **moon**.

sun   moon

44 — Fly and Monkey
Draw a line from the pictures that end with the **long i** sound to the **fly**.
Draw a line from the pictures that end with the **long e** sound to the **monkey**.

fly   monkey

46 — Animals! Animals!
Say the name for each animal.
Write the first letter to complete each word.

snake   bird   pig   rabbit   dog   lizard   cat   frog   turtle

48 — Who Made the Mess?
Say the word for each picture.
Complete the words with consonants from the clue list.

box   bed   lamp   bus   book   CLUES k x p d g n s   corn   dog

50 — Whales and Snails
Complete each sentence with one of these **long a** words:

snail, rain, whale
paint, drain, plains

We want to **paint** the fence red.

Zebras roam the Kenyan **plains**.

A **snail** moves very slowly.

Water goes down the **drain**.

The blue **whale** is the largest animal on Earth.

Hummingbirds drink drops of **rain**.

52 — Trees and Leaves
Complete each sentence with one of these **long e** words:

queen, bee, wheel
peach, feet, seal

Watch out! That **bee** might sting you.

I have ten toes on my **feet**.

The **seal** plays in the waves.

My favorite dessert is peach **pie**.

The **queen** wears a crown.

The **wheel** goes round and round.

54 — A Day at the Park
Complete each sentence with one of these **long i** words:

bike, fly, pie
sky, tie, slide

Amy rides a **bike**.

Lori goes down the **slide**.

Rico eats the **pie**.

Cody wears a **tie**.

There are no clouds in the **sky**.

The bees live in a **hive**.

The **fly** is buzzing around.

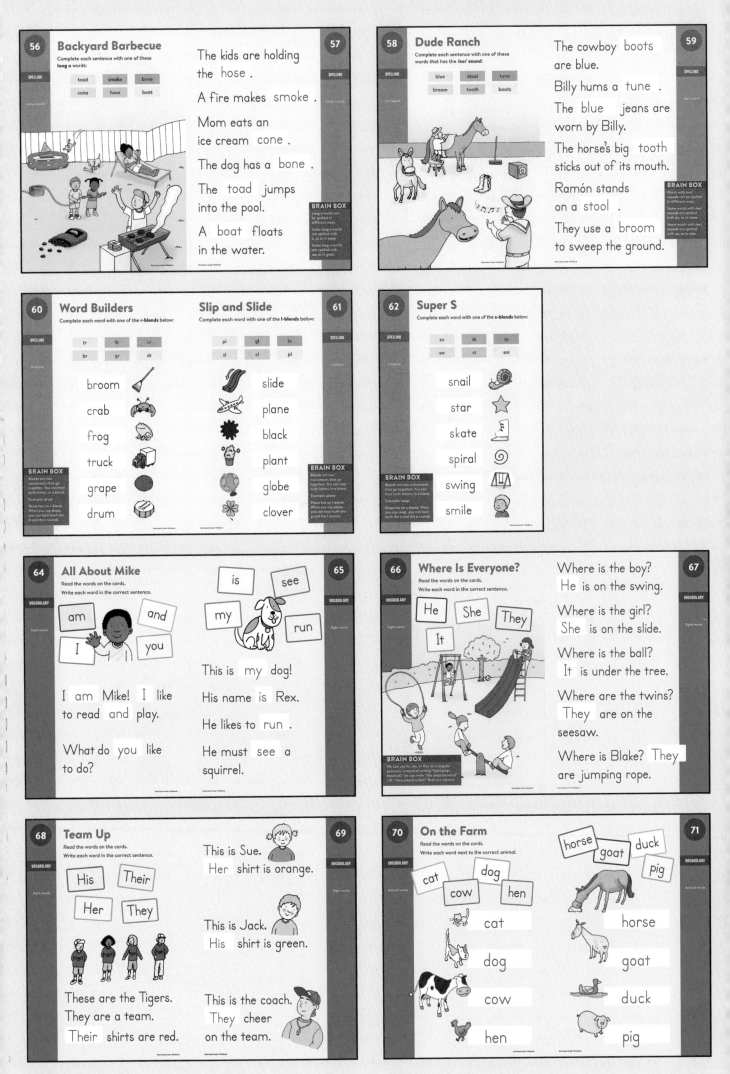

56 — Backyard Barbecue

SPELLING · Long o words

Complete each sentence with one of these **long o** words:

toad · smoke · bone · cone · hose · boat

The kids are holding the hose.

A fire makes smoke.

Mom eats an ice cream cone.

The dog has a bone.

The toad jumps into the pool.

A boat floats in the water.

BRAIN BOX
Long o words can be spelled in different ways. Some long o words are spelled with a, e, as in hose. Some long o words are spelled with oa, as in goat.

57 · SPELLING · Long o words

58 — Dude Ranch

SPELLING · /oo/ sound

Complete each sentence with one of these words that has the /oo/ sound:

blue · stool · tune · broom · tooth · boots

The cowboy boots are blue.

Billy hums a tune.

The blue jeans are worn by Billy.

The horse's big tooth sticks out of its mouth.

Ramón stands on a stool.

They use a broom to sweep the ground.

BRAIN BOX
Words with /oo/ sounds can be spelled in different ways. Some words with /oo/ sounds are spelled with oo, or in room. Some words with /oo/ sounds are spelled with ue, as in clue.

59 · SPELLING · /oo/ sound

60 — Word Builders

SPELLING · R-blends

Complete each word with one of the **r-blends** below:

tr · fr · cr · br · gr · dr

broom

crab

frog

truck

grape

drum

BRAIN BOX
Blends are two consonants that go together. You can hear both letters in a blend.
Example: drum
Drum has an r-blend. When you say drum, you can hear both the d and the r sounds.

Slip and Slide — 61

Complete each word with one of the **l-blends** below:

pl · gl · bl · sl · cl · pl

slide

plane

black

plant

globe

clover

BRAIN BOX
Blends are two consonants that go together. You can hear both letters in a blend.
Example: plane
Plane has an l-blend. When you say plane, you can hear both the p and the l sounds.

61 · SPELLING · L-blends

62 — Super S

SPELLING · S-blends

Complete each word with one of the **s-blends** below:

sn · sk · sp · sw · st · sm

snail

star

skate

spiral

swing

smile

BRAIN BOX
Blends are two consonants that go together. You can hear both letters in a blend.
Example: snap
Snap has an s-blend. When you say snap, you can hear both the s and the n sounds.

64 — All About Mike

VOCABULARY · Sight words

Read the words on the cards.
Write each word in the correct sentence.

am · and · I · you

is · see · my · run

I am Mike! I like to read and play.

What do you like to do?

This is my dog!

His name is Rex.

He likes to run.

He must see a squirrel.

65 · VOCABULARY · Sight words

66 — Where Is Everyone?

VOCABULARY · Sight words

Read the words on the cards.
Write each word in the correct sentence.

He · She · They · It

Where is the boy?
He is on the swing.

Where is the girl?
She is on the slide.

Where is the ball?
It is under the tree.

Where are the twins?
They are on the seesaw.

Where is Blake? They are jumping rope.

BRAIN BOX
We can use he, she, or they as a singular pronoun. Instead of writing "Sybil plays baseball," we can write "She plays baseball." OR: "They play baseball." Both are correct.

67 · VOCABULARY · Sight words

68 — Team Up

VOCABULARY · Sight words

Read the words on the cards.
Write each word in the correct sentence.

His · Their · Her · They

These are the Tigers.
They are a team.
Their shirts are red.

This is Sue.
Her shirt is orange.

This is Jack.
His shirt is green.

This is the coach.
They cheer on the team.

69 · VOCABULARY · Sight words

70 — On the Farm

VOCABULARY · Animal words

Read the words on the cards.
Write each word next to the correct animal.

cat · dog · cow · hen · horse · goat · duck · pig

cat

dog

cow

hen

horse

goat

duck

pig

71 · VOCABULARY · Animal words

In the Kitchen

Read the words on the cards.

Draw a line from each card to the correct picture on the next page.

Kitchen words

bowl

pot

cup

spoon

sink

pan

Kitchen words

At the Farmers Market

Read the words on the cards.

Draw a line from each card to the correct food on the next page.

Food words

butter

pears

bread

cheese

apples

eggs

FARMERS MARKET

Food words

Color Splash!

Read the color words on the cards.

Color the card the right color.

Color words

green

red

blue

orange

purple

yellow

Write the color word below each color.

green | orange

purple | blue

red | yellow

Finger Counting

Read the number words on the cards.

Count the number of fingers each hand is holding up.

Draw a line from each card to the correct hand.

Number words

two

four

one

five

three

seven

nine

six

ten

eight

Number words

Activities!

Read the words on the cards.

Write each word in the correct sentence.

Action words

dance | sing

paint | read

I like to sing .

I like to paint .

We like to dance .

I like to read .

Soccer Stars!

Read the words on the cards.

Write each word in the correct sentence.

Action words

catch | cheer

kick | jog

We jog .

We kick .

We catch .

We cheer .

Let's Go!

Read the words on the cards.

Write each word next to the correct picture.

Transportation words

bike | bus

boat | car

plane | truck

train | van

car

boat

bike

bus

plane

truck

train

van

Transportation words

Time to Rhyme!

The words on the cards all rhyme with **brag**. Write each rhyming word next to the correct picture.

Rhyming words

tag | wag

bag | flag

tag

bag

flag

wag

The words on the cards all rhyme with **tan**. Write each rhyming word next to the correct picture.

pan | fan

can | man

man

fan

can

pan

BRAIN BOX

Rhyming words have the same middle and ending sounds.

Cat and bat are rhyming words.

Rhyming words

Keep Rhyming!

The words on the cards all rhyme with **cool**. Write each rhyming word under the correct picture.

Rhyming words

school | pool

stool | spool

spool | school

pool | stool

The words on the cards all rhyme with **tone**. Write each rhyming word under the correct picture.

bone | stone

phone | cone

bone | cone

stone | phone

Rhyming words

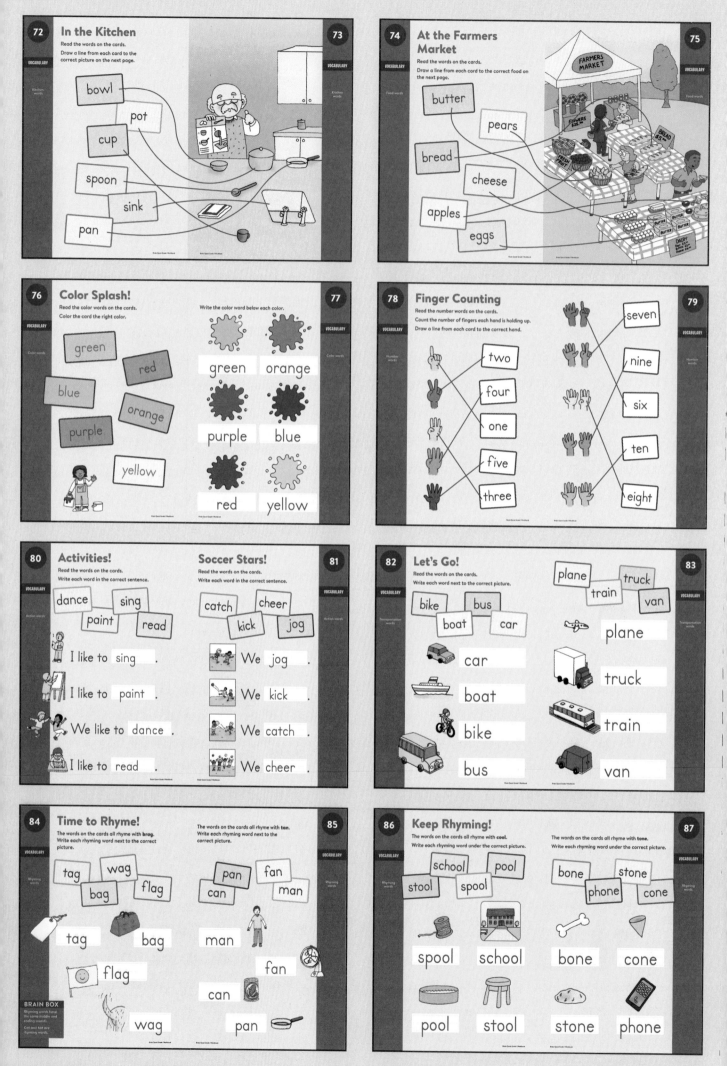

Our Pets

The words on the cards are the pet names.
Each pet's name rhymes with its owner's name.
Complete each sentence with the correct rhyming pet name.

Rhyming words

Nate   Harry   Spike

Sandy
Bailey   Dan

My name is Larry.
My dog is **Harry**.

My name is Kate.
My cat is **Nate**.

My name is Mike.
My dog is **Spike**.

Rhyming words

My name is Hailey.
My dog is **Bailey**.

My name is Andy.
My cat is **Sandy**.

My name is Jan.
My cat is **Dan**.

Find the Rhyme

Say the word for each picture.
Draw a line from each picture to
the word it rhymes with.

Rhyming words

vest

junk

feel

main

rice

People

Read the **nouns**.
They all name people.
Complete each sentence with the correct **noun** from the words below.

Nouns

daughter   boy   woman
father   veterinarian

BRAIN BOX
A noun is a word that names a person, place, or thing.

Nouns

The **veterinarian** examines the cat.

The **father** is wearing a brown sweater.

His **daughter** has pigtails.

The **boy** has brown hair.

The **woman** has a birdcage.

Animals

Read the **nouns**.
They all name animals.

Nouns

turtle   cat   bird   dog

BRAIN BOX
Animal words are nouns.

Complete each sentence with the correct **noun** from page 94.

Nouns

The **bird** chirps on a branch.

The **cat** hides behind the bush.

The **dog** walks on a leash.

The **turtle** rests on the rock.

Things

Read the **nouns**.
They all name things.

Nouns

hammer   nails   saw   wood

BRAIN BOX
Words for things are nouns.

Complete each sentence with the correct **noun** from page 96.

Nouns

José wants to build a birdhouse.

He has planks of **wood**.

He has a **saw** to cut the wood.

He has a box of **nails**.

The **hammer** is next to his sister.

Places

Read the **nouns**.
They all name places.

Nouns

beach   city   farm
forest   lake   town

Complete each sentence with the correct **noun** from page 98.

Nouns

We drive into **town**.

The boat floats on the **lake**.

The cow lives on the **farm**.

There are tall buildings in the **city**.

There is sand on the **beach**.

The **forest** has lots of trees.

BRAIN BOX
Words for places are nouns.

Go, Dino, Go!

Circle the **verb** in each sentence.

Verbs

The dinosaur (eats).

The dinosaur (hops).

The dinosaur (runs).

The dinosaur (hugs).

The dinosaur (sleeps).

The dinosaur (waves).

BRAIN BOX
A verb is an action word. A verb tells what someone or something does.
Example: The dinosaur sings.
In this sentence, sings is the verb. It tells what the dinosaur does.

Naming Feelings

Read the **adjectives**.
Write the correct **adjective** next to each friend to describe how they are feeling.

happy   confused   shy

confused

happy

shy

BRAIN BOX
An adjective is a describing word. It tells about or describes a noun.
Some adjectives tell what nouns look like.

worried   proud   unhappy

worried

proud

unhappy

104

Describe It!

Read the **adjectives**.
Write the correct **adjective** to tell about each animal.

pink   brown   red

white   green   gray

The **gray** elephant lives in Kenya.

The **white** polar bear lives in the Arctic.

The **green** lizard lives in the desert.

The **pink** flamingo lives near the water.

The **red** kangaroo lives in Australia.

The **brown** deer lives in the forest.

LANGUAGE ARTS

LANGUAGE ARTS

Cat Chase!

Read this **sentence**.

The (cat) naps△

Circle the **noun**.

Underline the **verb**.

Draw a box around the **capital letter** that begins the sentence.

Draw a triangle around the **period** that ends the sentence.

Now copy the **sentence** here.

The cat naps.

BRAIN BOX
A sentence is a group of words that express a complete thought.

All sentences begin with a capital letter.

A statement is a sentence that explains or tells what someone or something does.

A statement ends with a period.

Circle the **noun** in this sentence:

The (cat) wakes up.

Underline the **verb** in this sentence:

The cat runs.

Draw a box around the **capital letter** that begins this sentence:

The dog chases the cat.

Draw a triangle around the **period** that ends this sentence:

The dog naps△

LANGUAGE ARTS

LANGUAGE ARTS

Superstar!

These sentences are written wrong.
Write each sentence correctly.

the cow sings.
The cow sings.

the cow dances
The cow dances.

the cow acts
The cow acts.

The receives cow flowers.
The cow receives flowers.

cow bows. The
The cow bows.

waves The cow
The cow waves.

BRAIN BOX
A statement begins with a capital letter.
A statement ends with a period.

LANGUAGE ARTS

LANGUAGE ARTS

So Many Questions!

These questions are written wrong.
Write each sentence correctly.

how do you feel
How do you feel?

who is your best friend
Who is your best friend?

when is your next show
When is your next show?

what is your favorite song
What is your favorite song?

BRAIN BOX
Sentences that ask for information are called questions.

A question begins with a capital letter.

This is a question mark, ?.

A question ends with a question mark.

More Dessert, Please?

Read each **question**.
Circle the question word.

(What) kind of dessert is it?

(Who) made the dessert?

(Where) is the dessert?

(When) was the dessert ready?

(Why) did they make the dessert?

(How) does it taste?

BRAIN BOX
Questions start with question words.
Who, what, where, when, why, and how are all question words.

LANGUAGE ARTS

LANGUAGE ARTS

She Makes Pizza

Add the letter **s** to each verb to tell what is happening now.

She roll **s** out the pizza dough.

She pour **s** the sauce.

She sprinkle **s** the cheese.

She put **s** the pizza in the oven.

She take **s** out the pizza.

BRAIN BOX
A present-tense verb tells what is happening now.
You can add the letter s to many verbs to tell about what is happening now.

They Planted Flowers!

Add the letters **ed** to each verb to tell what happened in the past.

They want **ed** to plant flowers.

She gather **ed** the seeds.

He turn **ed** over the soil.

They pour **ed** the seeds in the ground.

He water **ed** the seeds.

BRAIN BOX
A past-tense verb tells what happened in the past.
You can add ed to many verbs to tell about actions that happened in the past.

LANGUAGE ARTS

LANGUAGE ARTS

The More the Merrier!

Look at the picture. Complete each sentence using the word **is** or **are**.

The monkeys **are** climbing.

The elephant **is** spraying.

The lions **are** roaring.

The giraffe **is** eating.

The zebra **is** dancing.

The hippos **are** singing.

LANGUAGE ARTS

LANGUAGE ARTS

Fresh Foods

Write the plural for each food word by adding the letter **s** at the end of the word.

pumpkin   pumpkins

pepper   peppers

carrot   carrots

apple   apples

BRAIN BOX
Plural means there is more than one.
You can add an s to make most nouns plural.

READING

Drake the Dragon

Read about Drake.
Then answer the questions.

This is Drake.
Drake is a dragon.
Drake is purple.
Drake lives in a cave.
Drake lives with a snake.
Drake and the snake are best friends.

What is Drake?
Drake is a **dragon**.

What color is Drake?
Drake is **purple**.

Where does Drake live?
Drake lives in a **cave**.

Who is Drake's best friend?
Drake's best friend is a **snake**.

READING

Picking Apples

Read about apples.
Then answer the questions.

Apples grow on trees.
You can pick apples in the fall.
This family is picking red apples.

Where do apples grow?

Apples grow on trees .

When can you pick apples?

You can pick apples in the
fall .

What color are the apples
on the trees?

The apples are red .

Camp Out

Read about the camping trip.
Number the pictures from 1 to 4 to
show what happens in order.

1. We find a spot by the river.
2. We set up our tents.
3. We get some sticks for a fire.
4. We make dinner and sing!

3
2
4
1

Robot Race

Read about Robbie.
Then answer the questions.

Robbie is a robot.
Robbie is in a race.
Robbie has wheels for feet!
Robbie rolls fast.
He rolls past the other robots.
Robbie wins the race!

What is Robbie?

Robbie is a robot .

What does Robbie have
for feet?

Robbie has wheels .

Who wins
the race?

Robbie
wins the race.

Draw your own robot here!

Understanding Feelings

Read the sentences.
Choose the correct word to tell how each person
feels. Write it on the line.

Tamiko can't wait to play soccer.

Tamiko is
excited
excited   upset

Max is
sleepy
sleepy   mad

Max just got home from a long trip.

Pilar is reading a book before bed.

Pilar is
focused
sad   focused

Leo is a new student at school.

Leo is
nervous
angry   nervous

Jamal just found his lost dog!

Jamal is
happy
happy   frustrated

Nora is
proud
proud   disappointed

Nora just won the school spelling bee!

BRAIN BOX

Using specific words to explain our emotions helps us express how we are feeling. This builds our emotional vocabulary and allows us to be understood more clearly.

Plants!

Read about plants.

Flowers are plants.
Trees are plants.
Grass is a plant, too.
Rocks are not plants.
Water is not a plant.
The rabbit is not a plant.

Color the cards with plant words **green**.

rocks
rabbit
trees
grass
flowers
water

Omar at the Beach

Omar went to the beach.
He saw sand.
He saw water.
He saw a crab.
He got hit by a wave. Omar got wet!

What did Omar see at the
beach?

He saw sand.

He saw water.

He saw a crab.

Draw what you would pack for a day at the beach.

Monster Music!

Read each sentence.
Then draw a line to the matching picture.

Molly plays
the drums.

Michael plays
the tuba.

Mark plays
the violin.

Maria plays
the flute.

If you were a monster, what would you play?

I would play the

Draw yourself playing your instrument.

The Witch's Spell

Read about the witch.
Number the pictures from 1 to 5 to
show what happens in order.

1. Wilma the Witch has a frog.
2. She turns the frog into a bird!
3. She turns the bird into a bug!
4. She turns the bug into a dog!
5. She turns the dog into a frog again.

2
4
1
5
3

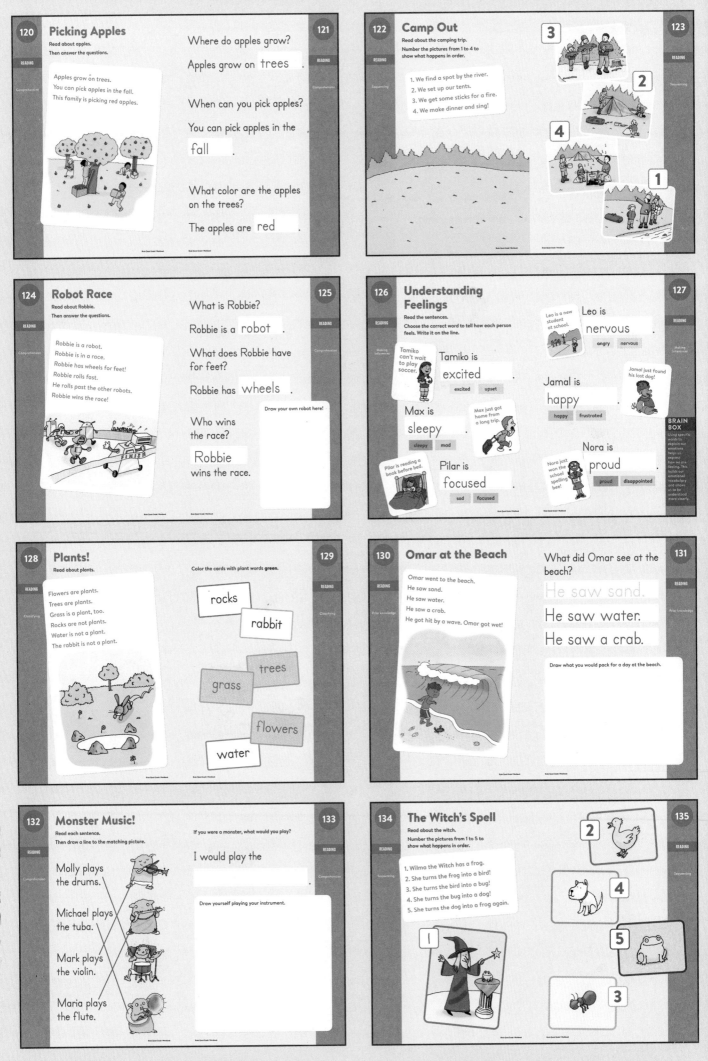

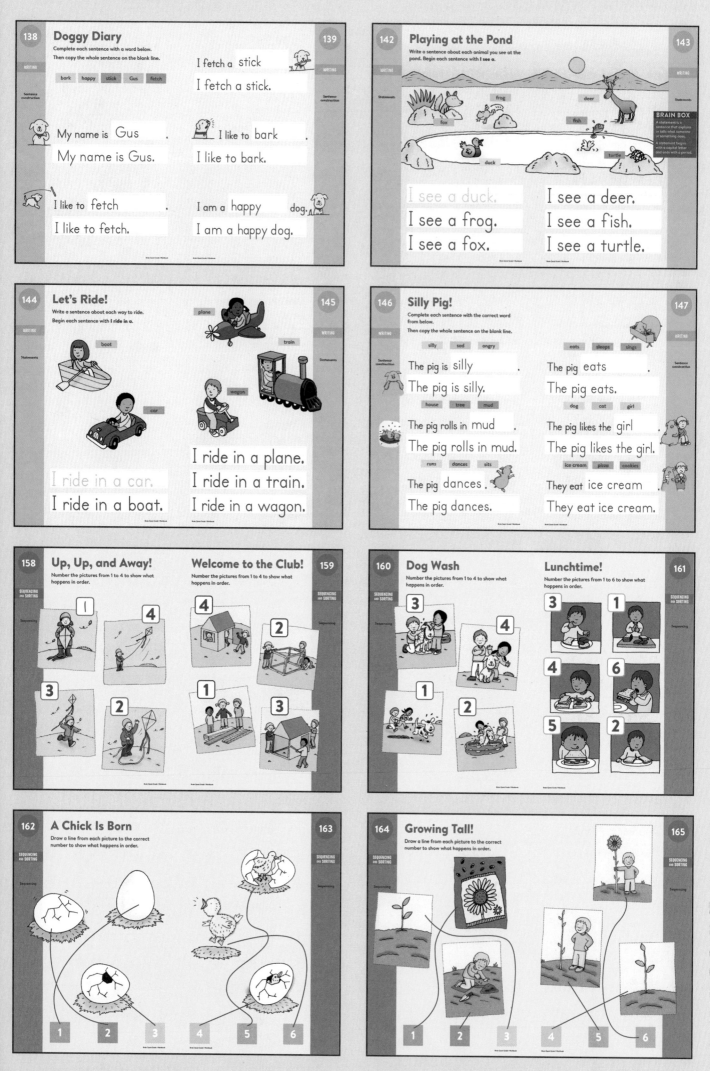

Doggy Diary

Complete each sentence with a word below.
Then copy the whole sentence on the blank line.

bark   happy   stick   Gus   fetch

I fetch a stick
I fetch a stick.

My name is Gus .
My name is Gus.

I like to bark
I like to bark.

I like to fetch .
I like to fetch.

I am a happy dog.
I am a happy dog.

Playing at the Pond

Write a sentence about each animal you see at the pond. Begin each sentence with I see a.

fox   frog   deer   fish   duck   turtle

BRAIN BOX
A statement is a sentence that explains or tells what someone or something does.
A statement begins with a capital letter and ends with a period.

I see a duck.
I see a frog.
I see a fox.

I see a deer.
I see a fish.
I see a turtle.

Let's Ride!

Write a sentence about each way to ride.
Begin each sentence with I ride in a.

boat   plane   train   car   wagon

I ride in a car.
I ride in a boat.

I ride in a plane.
I ride in a train.
I ride in a wagon.

Silly Pig!

Complete each sentence with the correct word from below.
Then copy the whole sentence on the blank line.

silly   sad   angry

The pig is silly
The pig is silly.

house   tree   mud

The pig rolls in mud
The pig rolls in mud.

runs   dances   sits

The pig dances .
The pig dances.

eats   sleeps   sings

The pig eats
The pig eats.

dog   cat   girl

The pig likes the girl
The pig likes the girl.

ice cream   pizza   cookies

They eat ice cream .
They eat ice cream.

Up, Up, and Away!

Number the pictures from 1 to 4 to show what happens in order.

Welcome to the Club!

Number the pictures from 1 to 4 to show what happens in order.

Dog Wash

Number the pictures from 1 to 4 to show what happens in order.

Lunchtime!

Number the pictures from 1 to 6 to show what happens in order.

A Chick Is Born

Draw a line from each picture to the correct number to show what happens in order.

1   2   3   4   5   6

Growing Tall!

Draw a line from each picture to the correct number to show what happens in order.

1   2   3   4   5   6

Brain Quest Grade 1 Workbook

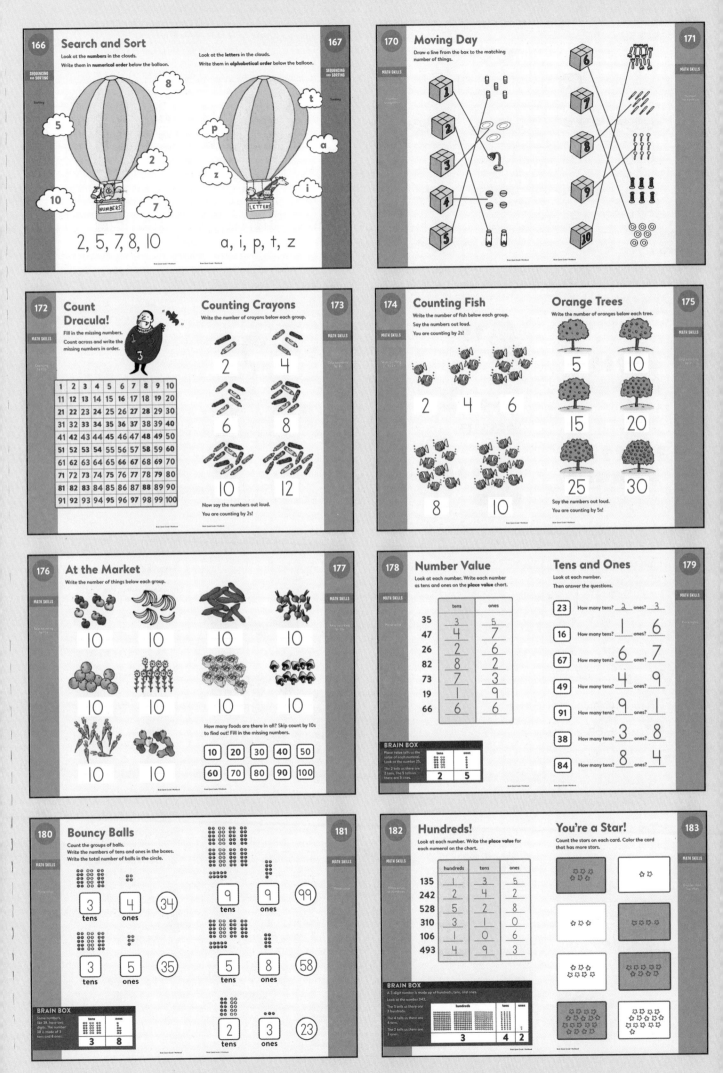

166 Search and Sort

SEQUENCING AND SORTING

Look at the **numbers** in the clouds.
Write them in **numerical order** below the balloon.

8
5
2
10
7

NUMBERS

2, 5, 7, 8, 10

167

SEQUENCING AND SORTING

Look at the **letters** in the clouds.
Write them in **alphabetical order** below the balloon.

t
p
a
z
i

LETTERS

a, i, p, t, z

170 Moving Day

MATH SKILLS

Draw a line from the box to the matching number of things.

1
2
3
4
5
6
7
8
9
10

172 Count Dracula!

MATH SKILLS

Fill in the missing numbers.
Count across and write the missing numbers in order.

1	2	3	4	5	6	7	8	9	10
11	12	13	14	15	16	17	18	19	20
21	22	23	24	25	26	27	28	29	30
31	32	33	34	35	36	37	38	39	40
41	42	43	44	45	46	47	48	49	50
51	52	53	54	55	56	57	58	59	60
61	62	63	64	65	66	67	68	69	70
71	72	73	74	75	76	77	78	79	80
81	82	83	84	85	86	87	88	89	90
91	92	93	94	95	96	97	98	99	100

Counting Crayons

173

MATH SKILLS

Write the number of crayons below each group.

2
4
6
8
10
12

Now say the numbers out loud.
You are counting by 2s!

174 Counting Fish

MATH SKILLS

Write the number of fish below each group.
Say the numbers out loud.
You are counting by 2s!

2
4
6
8
10

Orange Trees

175

MATH SKILLS

Write the number of oranges below each tree.

5
10
15
20
25
30

Say the numbers out loud.
You are counting by 5s!

176 At the Market

MATH SKILLS

Write the number of things below each group.

10 10 10 10
10 10 10 10
10 10

How many foods are there in all? Skip count by 10s to find out! Fill in the missing numbers.

| 10 | 20 | 30 | 40 | 50 |
| 60 | 70 | 80 | 90 | 100 |

178 Number Value

MATH SKILLS

Look at each number. Write each number as tens and ones on the **place value** chart.

	tens	ones
35	3	5
47	4	7
26	2	6
82	8	2
73	7	3
19	1	9
66	6	6

BRAIN BOX
Place value tells us the value of each numeral. Look at the number 25.
The 2 tells us there are 2 tens, the 5 tells us there are 5 ones.

tens	ones
2	5

Tens and Ones

179

MATH SKILLS

Look at each number.
Then answer the questions.

23 How many tens? 2 ones? 3
16 How many tens? 1 ones? 6
67 How many tens? 6 ones? 7
49 How many tens? 4 ones? 9
91 How many tens? 9 ones? 1
38 How many tens? 3 ones? 8
84 How many tens? 8 ones? 4

180 Bouncy Balls

MATH SKILLS

Count the groups of balls.
Write the numbers of tens and ones in the boxes.
Write the total number of balls in the circle.

3 tens   4 ones   34
3 tens   5 ones   35
2 tens   3 ones   23

BRAIN BOX
Some numbers, like 38, have two digits. The number 38 is made of 3 tens and 8 ones.

tens	ones
3	8

181

MATH SKILLS

9 tens   9 ones   99
5 tens   8 ones   58

182 Hundreds!

MATH SKILLS

Look at each number. Write the **place value** for each numeral on the chart.

	hundreds	tens	ones
135	1	3	5
242	2	4	2
528	5	2	8
310	3	1	0
106	1	0	6
493	4	9	3

BRAIN BOX
A 3-digit number is made up of hundreds, tens, and ones. Look at the number 342.
The 3 tells us there are 3 hundreds.
The 4 tells us there are 4 tens.
The 2 tells us there are 2 ones.

hundreds	tens	ones
3	4	2

You're a Star!

183

MATH SKILLS

Count the stars on each card. Color the card that has more stars.

Bake Sale

Count the brownies on each plate.
Write the number in the box below the brownies.
Then write < or > to show which plate has more brownies.

8 > 6

5 > 3

8 < 10

2 < 7

3 > 1

BRAIN BOX
< means less than.
> means greater than.

Brick by Brick

Look at the brick towers.

Circle the tower with the **most** bricks.
Put an X on the tower with the **fewest** bricks.

Circle the tower with the **most** bricks.
Put an X on the tower with the **fewest** bricks.

Circle the towers with the **same number** of bricks.
Put an X on the tower with the **fewest** bricks.

Circle the towers with the **same number** of bricks.
Put an X on the tower with the **fewest** bricks.

Award Winners!

For each ribbon, color a block on the bar.
Circle the animal that won the most ribbons.

Book Worm

How many books do you think you see?
Don't count them. Just take a guess!

Write the number you guessed:

Good job! You **estimated**!
Now count the books.
Write the number you counted: 19
Were you close?

Pot of Gold

How many gold coins do you think you see?
Don't count them. Just take a guess!

Write the number you guessed:

Good job! You **estimated**!
Now count the coins.
Write the number you counted: 23
Were you close?

Snow Day!

How many snowflakes do you think you see?
Don't count them. Just take a guess!
Write the number you guessed:

Now count the snowflakes.
Write the number you counted: 16
Were you close?

Play Ball!

Count the balls in each group.
Write the number in the box below.
Write the **sum** in the colored box.

3 + 2 = 5

1 + 3 = 4

8 = 5 + 3

Star Search

Count the stars in each group.
Write the number in the box below.
Write the **sum** in the colored box.

2 + 6 = 8

9 = 4 + 5

7 + 1 = 8

BRAIN BOX
You add to find out how many things there are altogether.
Example: 2 + 3 = 5
Here, we are adding the numbers 2 and 3. We use a + sign to show addition.
5 is how many we have altogether. This is called the sum. We use an = sign to show that the value on both sides is the same.

At the Toy Store

Count the toys in each group.
Write the number in the box below.
Add the numbers. Write the **sum** in the colored box.

5 + 3 = 8

4 + 2 = 6

7 = 1 + 6

7 + 5 = 12

7 = 3 + 4

1 + 2 = 3

Super Scoops!

Count the scoops on each cone.
Write each number in the box.
Add the numbers to find out how many scoops there are in all.
Write the **sum** in the box below the line.

4
+ 3
___
7

5
+ 2
___
7

BRAIN BOX
Addition sentences can be written two ways:

3 + 1 = 4

3
+ 1
___
4

Pancake Party!

Count the pancakes on each plate.
Write each number in the box.
Add the numbers to find out how many pancakes there are in all.
Write the **sum** in the box below the line.

6
+ 7
___
13

5
+ 10
___
15

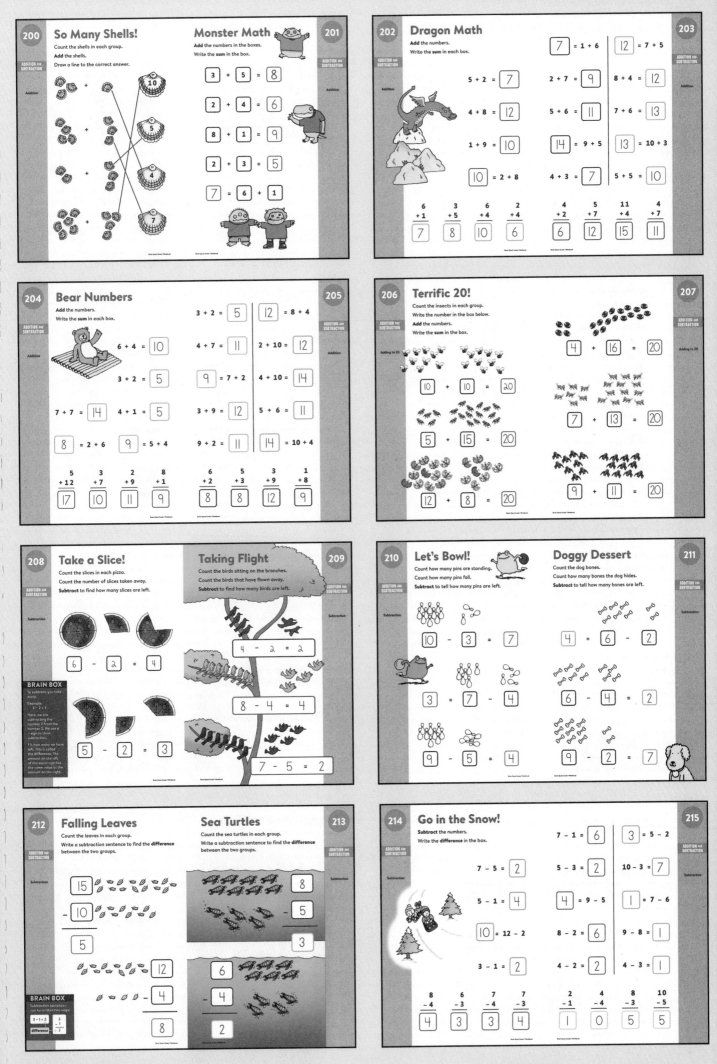

200 — So Many Shells!

Count the shells in each group.
Add the shells.
Draw a line to the correct answer.

201 — Monster Math

Add the numbers in the boxes.
Write the **sum** in the box.

$3 + 5 = 8$

$2 + 4 = 6$

$8 + 1 = 9$

$2 + 3 = 5$

$7 = 6 + 1$

202 / 203 — Dragon Math

Add the numbers.
Write the **sum** in each box.

$7 = 1 + 6$ | $12 = 7 + 5$

$5 + 2 = 7$ | $2 + 7 = 9$ | $8 + 4 = 12$

$4 + 8 = 12$ | $5 + 6 = 11$ | $7 + 6 = 13$

$1 + 9 = 10$ | $14 = 9 + 5$ | $13 = 10 + 3$

$10 = 2 + 8$ | $4 + 3 = 7$ | $5 + 5 = 10$

6	3	6	2	4	5	11	4
$+1$	$+5$	$+4$	$+4$	$+2$	$+7$	$+4$	$+7$
7	8	10	6	6	12	15	11

204 / 205 — Bear Numbers

Add the numbers.
Write the **sum** in each box.

$3 + 2 = 5$ | $12 = 8 + 4$

$6 + 4 = 10$ | $4 + 7 = 11$ | $2 + 10 = 12$

$3 + 2 = 5$ | $9 = 7 + 2$ | $4 + 10 = 14$

$7 + 7 = 14$ | $4 + 1 = 5$ | $3 + 9 = 12$ | $5 + 6 = 11$

$8 = 2 + 6$ | $9 = 5 + 4$ | $9 + 2 = 11$ | $14 = 10 + 4$

5	3	2	8	6	5	3	1
$+12$	$+7$	$+9$	$+1$	$+2$	$+3$	$+9$	$+8$
17	10	11	9	8	8	12	9

206 / 207 — Terrific 20!

Count the insects in each group.
Write the number in the box below.
Add the numbers.
Write the **sum** in the box.

$10 + 10 = 20$

$5 + 15 = 20$

$12 + 8 = 20$

$4 + 16 = 20$

$7 + 13 = 20$

$9 + 11 = 20$

208 — Take a Slice!

Count the slices in each pizza.
Count the number of slices taken away.
Subtract to find how many slices are left.

$6 - 2 = 4$

$5 - 2 = 3$

BRAIN BOX
To subtract, you take away.
Example:
$3 - 2 = 1$
Here, we are subtracting the number 2 from the number 3. We use a − sign to show subtraction.

1 is how many we have left. This is called the difference. The amount on the left of the equal sign has the same value as the amount on the right.

209 — Taking Flight

Count the birds sitting on the branches.
Count the birds that have flown away.
Subtract to find how many birds are left.

$4 - 2 = 2$

$8 - 4 = 4$

$7 - 5 = 2$

210 — Let's Bowl!

Count how many pins are standing.
Count how many pins fall.
Subtract to tell how many pins are left.

$10 - 3 = 7$

$3 = 7 - 4$

$9 - 5 = 4$

211 — Doggy Dessert

Count the dog bones.
Count how many bones the dog hides.
Subtract to tell how many bones are left.

$4 = 6 - 2$

$6 - 4 = 2$

$9 - 2 = 7$

212 — Falling Leaves

Count the leaves in each group.
Write a subtraction sentence to find the **difference** between the two groups.

$15 - 10 = 5$

$12 - 4 = 8$

BRAIN BOX
Subtraction sentences can be written two ways:
$3 - 1 = 2$
or
3
-1
2
difference

213 — Sea Turtles

Count the sea turtles in each group.
Write a subtraction sentence to find the **difference** between the two groups.

$8 - 5 = 3$

$6 - 4 = 2$

214 / 215 — Go in the Snow!

Subtract the numbers.
Write the **difference** in the box.

$7 - 1 = 6$ | $3 = 5 - 2$

$7 - 5 = 2$ | $5 - 3 = 2$ | $10 - 3 = 7$

$5 - 1 = 4$ | $4 = 9 - 5$ | $1 = 7 - 6$

$10 = 12 - 2$ | $8 - 2 = 6$ | $9 - 8 = 1$

$3 - 1 = 2$ | $4 - 2 = 2$ | $4 - 3 = 1$

8	6	7	7	2	4	8	10
-4	-3	-4	-3	-1	-4	-3	-5
4	3	3	4	1	0	5	5

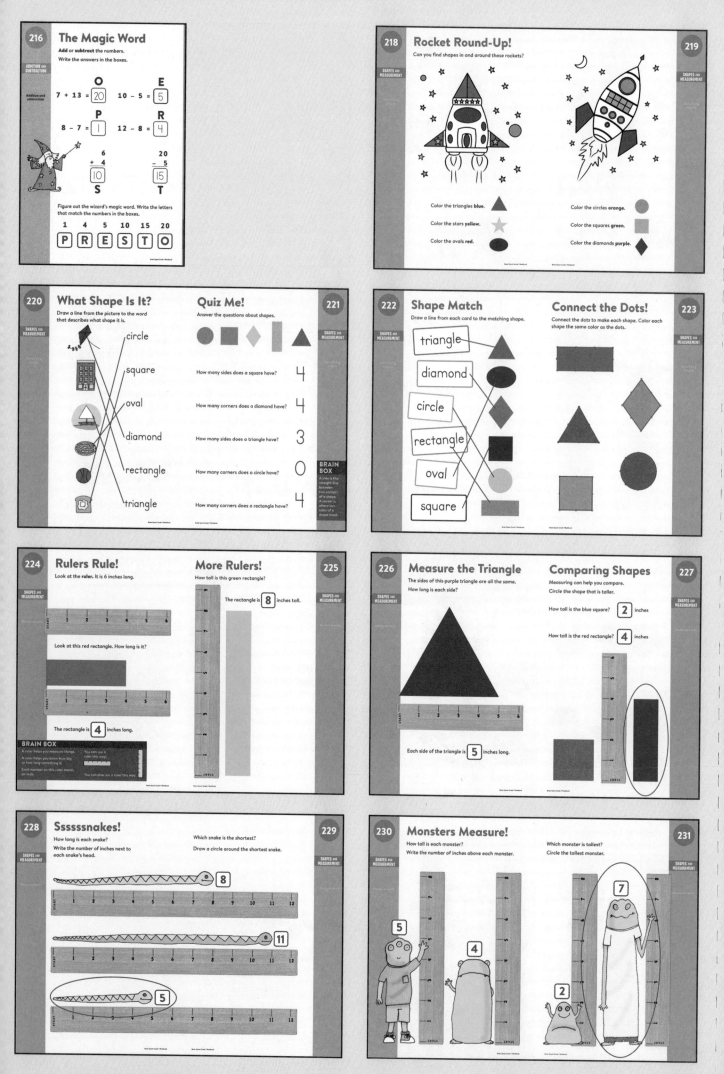

The Magic Word

Add or **subtract** the numbers.
Write the answers in the boxes.

O
7 + 13 = 20

E
10 − 5 = 5

P
8 − 7 = 1

R
12 − 8 = 4

```
    6
  + 4
  ────
   10
    S
```

```
   20
  − 5
  ────
   15
    T
```

Figure out the wizard's magic word. Write the letters
that match the numbers in the boxes.

1	4	5	10	15	20
P	R	E	S	T	O

Rocket Round-Up!

Can you find shapes in and around these rockets?

Color the triangles **blue**.
Color the stars **yellow**.
Color the ovals **red**.

Color the circles **orange**.
Color the squares **green**.
Color the diamonds **purple**.

What Shape Is It?

Draw a line from the picture to the word
that describes what shape it is.

- circle
- square
- oval
- diamond
- rectangle
- triangle

Quiz Me!

Answer the questions about shapes.

How many sides does a square have? **4**

How many corners does a diamond have? **4**

How many sides does a triangle have? **3**

How many corners does a circle have? **0**

How many corners does a rectangle have? **4**

BRAIN BOX
A side is the straight line between two corners of a shape. A corner is where two sides of a shape meet.

Shape Match

Draw a line from each card to the matching shape.

- triangle
- diamond
- circle
- rectangle
- oval
- square

Connect the Dots!

Connect the dots to make each shape. Color each
shape the same color as the dots.

Rulers Rule!

Look at the **ruler**. It is 6 inches long.

Look at this red rectangle. How long is it?

The rectangle is **4** inches long.

BRAIN BOX
A ruler helps you measure things.
A ruler helps you know how big or how long something is.
Each number on this ruler marks an inch.

You can use a ruler this way:
You can also use a ruler this way:

More Rulers!

How tall is this green rectangle?

The rectangle is **8** inches tall.

Measure the Triangle

The sides of this purple triangle are all the same.
How long is each side?

Each side of the triangle is **5** inches long.

Comparing Shapes

Measuring can help you compare.
Circle the shape that is taller.

How tall is the blue square? **2** inches

How tall is the red rectangle? **4** inches

Sssssssnakes!

How long is each snake?
Write the number of inches next to
each snake's head.

8

11

5

Which snake is the shortest?
Draw a circle around the shortest snake.

Monsters Measure!

How tall is each monster?
Write the number of inches above each monster.

5

4

Which monster is tallest?
Circle the tallest monster.

7

2

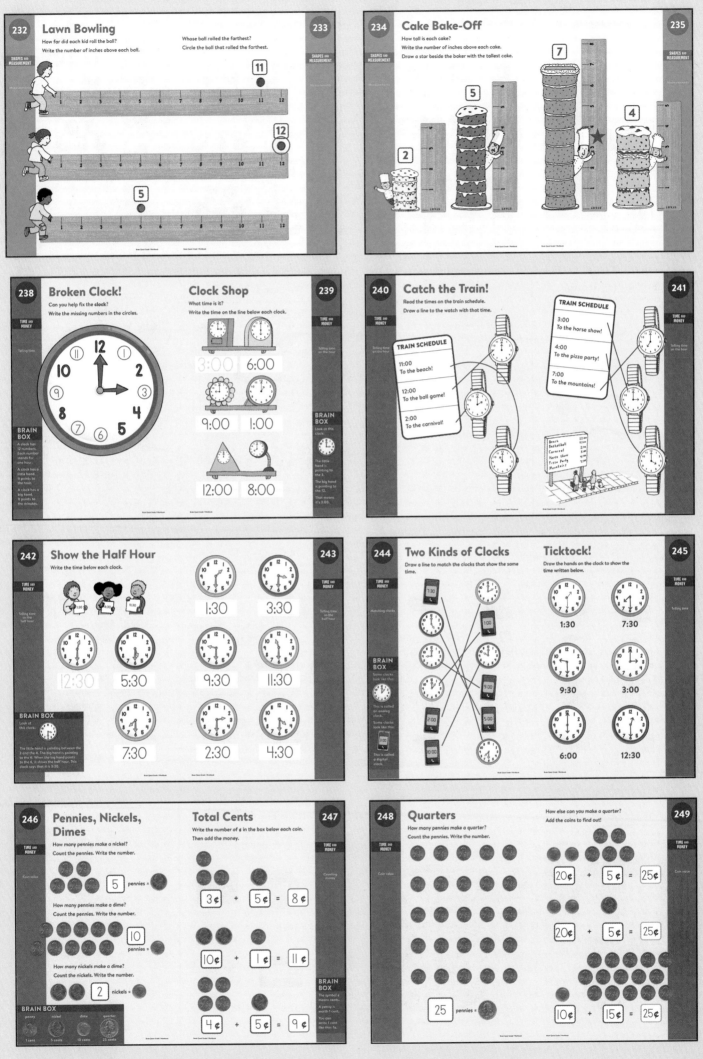

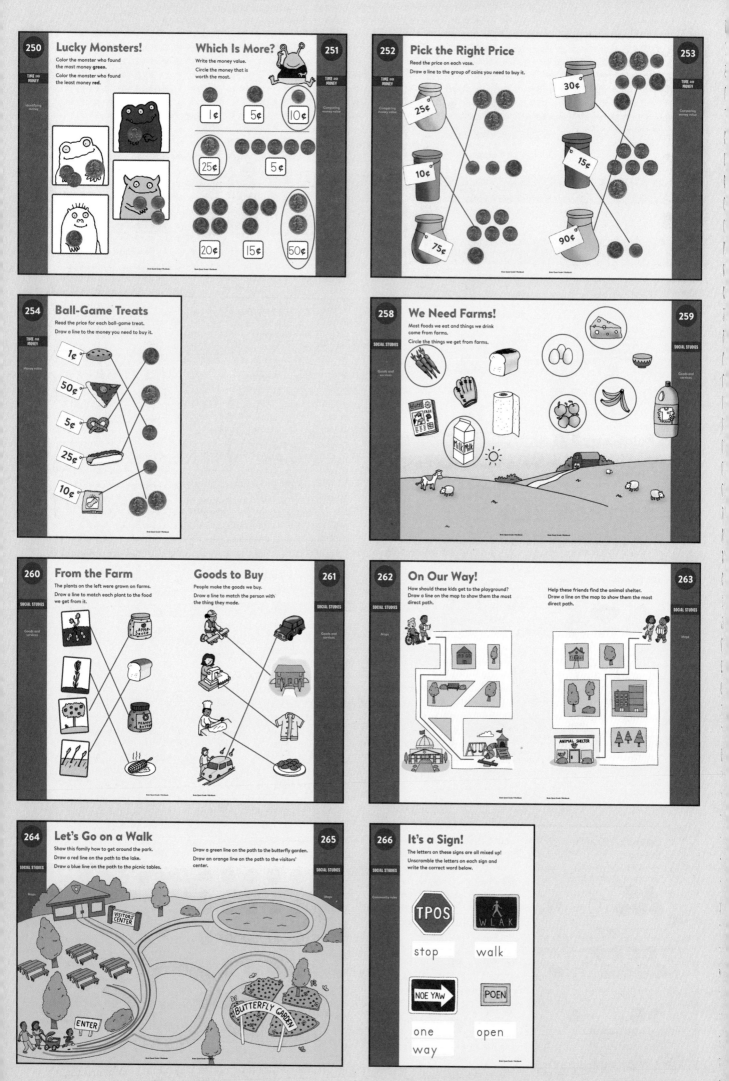

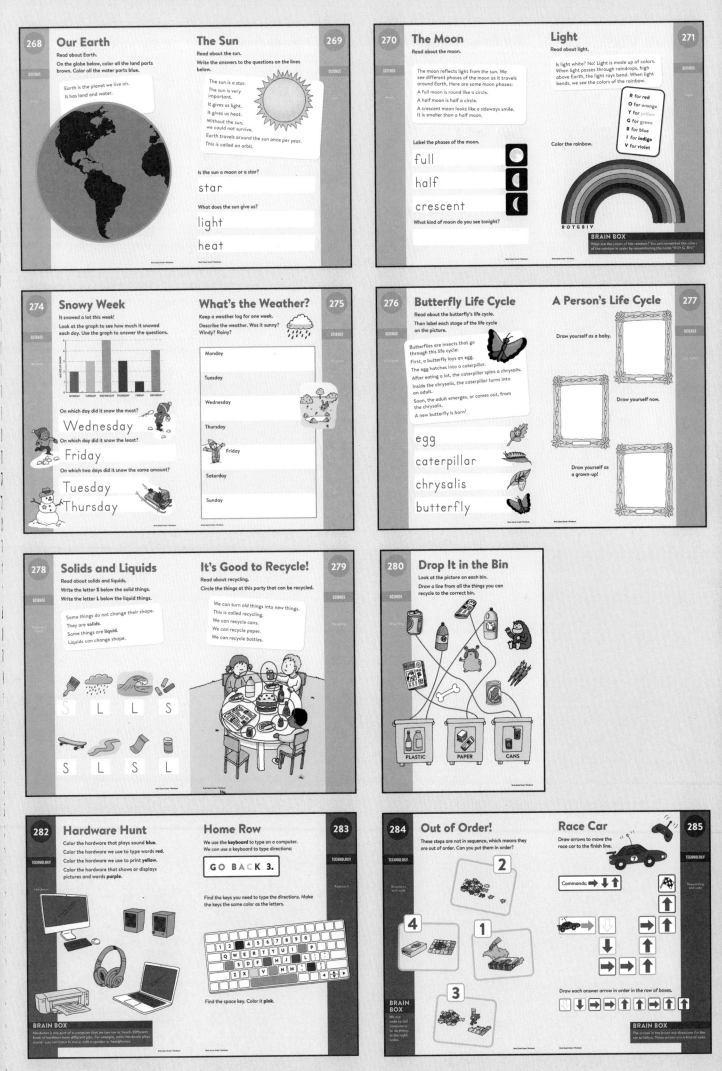

268 — Our Earth
SCIENCE

Read about Earth.
On the globe below, color all the land parts brown. Color all the water parts blue.

Earth is the planet we live on.
It has land and water.

The Sun — 269
SCIENCE

Read about the sun.
Write the answers to the questions on the lines below.

The sun is a star.
The sun is very important.
It gives us light.
It gives us heat.
Without the sun, we could not survive.
Earth travels around the sun once per year.
This is called an orbit.

Is the sun a moon or a star?

star

What does the sun give us?

light

heat

270 — The Moon
SCIENCE

Read about the moon.

The moon reflects light from the sun. We see different phases of the moon as it travels around Earth. Here are some moon phases:
A full moon is round like a circle.
A half moon is half a circle.
A crescent moon looks like a sideways smile. It is smaller than a half moon.

Label the phases of the moon.

full

half

crescent

What kind of moon do you see tonight?

Light — 271
SCIENCE

Read about light.

Is light white? No! Light is made up of colors. When light passes through raindrops, high above Earth, the light rays bend. When light bends, we see the colors of the rainbow.

R for red
O for orange
Y for yellow
G for green
B for blue
I for indigo
V for violet

Color the rainbow.

ROYGBIV

BRAIN BOX
What are the colors of the rainbow? You can remember the colors of the rainbow in order by remembering the name "ROY G. BIV."

274 — Snowy Week
SCIENCE

It snowed a lot this week!
Look at the graph to see how much it snowed each day. Use the graph to answer the questions.

On which day did it snow the most?

Wednesday

On which day did it snow the least?

Friday

On which two days did it snow the same amount?

Tuesday
Thursday

What's the Weather? — 275
SCIENCE

Keep a weather log for one week.
Describe the weather. Was it sunny? Windy? Rainy?

Monday
Tuesday
Wednesday
Thursday
Friday
Saturday
Sunday

276 — Butterfly Life Cycle
SCIENCE

Read about the butterfly's life cycle.
Then label each stage of the life cycle on the picture.

Butterflies are insects that go through this life cycle:
First, a butterfly lays an egg.
The egg hatches into a caterpillar.
After eating a lot, the caterpillar spins a chrysalis.
Inside the chrysalis, the caterpillar turns into an adult.
Soon, the adult emerges, or comes out, from the chrysalis.
A new butterfly is born!

egg

caterpillar

chrysalis

butterfly

A Person's Life Cycle — 277
SCIENCE

Draw yourself as a baby.

Draw yourself now.

Draw yourself as a grown-up!

278 — Solids and Liquids
SCIENCE

Read about solids and liquids.
Write the letter S below the solid things.
Write the letter L below the liquid things.

Some things do not change their shape.
They are solids.
Some things are liquid.
Liquids can change shape.

S L L S

S L S L

It's Good to Recycle! — 279
SCIENCE

Read about recycling.
Circle the things at this party that can be recycled.

We can turn old things into new things.
This is called recycling.
We can recycle cans.
We can recycle paper.
We can recycle bottles.

280 — Drop It in the Bin
SCIENCE

Look at the picture on each bin.
Draw a line from all the things you can recycle to the correct bin.

PLASTIC   PAPER   CANS

282 — Hardware Hunt
TECHNOLOGY

Color the hardware that plays sound blue.
Color the hardware we use to type words red.
Color the hardware we use to print yellow.
Color the hardware that shows or displays pictures and words purple.

BRAIN BOX
Hardware is any part of a computer that we can see or touch. Different kinds of hardware have different jobs. For example, some hardware plays sound—you can listen to music with a speaker or headphones.

Home Row — 283
TECHNOLOGY

We use the keyboard to type on a computer.
We can use a keyboard to type directions:

GO BACK 3.

Find the keys you need to type the directions. Make the keys the same color as the letters.

Find the space key. Color it pink.

284 — Out of Order!
TECHNOLOGY

These steps are not in sequence, which means they are out of order. Can you put them in order?

2

4   1

3

BRAIN BOX
We use code to tell computers to do things in the right order.

Race Car — 285
TECHNOLOGY

Draw arrows to move the race car to the finish line.

Commands: → ↓ ↑

Draw each answer arrow in order in the row of boxes.

BRAIN BOX
The arrows in the boxes are directions for the car to follow. These arrows are a kind of code.

Pick a Path!

The mouse can take two paths to get home.
One is yellow. The other is green.

Draw arrows in the boxes for each path.

Choices: ➡️ ⬇️ ⬅️

Circle the path that is shorter.

NOTE: If a box has two colors, then both paths can cross through it.

New Battery

Help the robot reach the battery.

In order, draw each arrow you see in the box below into each box of the path.

➡️ ⬇️ ⬇️ ⬇️ ⬇️ ⬅️ ⬅️ ➡️

Oops! There's a mistake. Circle the bug. Draw the correct arrow in this box.

➡️

BRAIN BOX

A mistake in a computer program is called a bug.

Favorite Fruit

Jamal and his friends love fruit. Each ❤️ shows a friend's favorite fruit.

🍎 🍌 🍇

BRAIN BOX

Computer programs use numbers or other symbols to represent information.

Circle the fruit that the friends like most.

Put an **X** through the fruit they like least.

Draw a square around your favorite fruit!

Fall Leaves

Color the leaves. Count each kind.

Make a bar graph. Color one box to represent one leaf.

Hello, Robot!

The robot has a secret message for you. Use the key to see what it says!

KEY

When you see . . .	★	💧	❀	✿	❁	✎
Write the letter	O	A	I	N	E	C	D

I CAN

CODE!

BRAIN QUEST
EXTRAS

You did it! Time to make a Brain Quest Mini-Deck so you can play and learn wherever you go. Fill out your certificate and hang your poster. Great work!

PARENTS Congratulations to you and your child. In this section you can help your child cut out the Brain Quest Mini-Deck and certificate and hang up their poster. Continue to make learning part of your everyday life beyond this book. Read aloud to your child as much as you can, search for numbers on outings, and keep asking questions to encourage their curiosity and extend their learning.

CONGRATULATIONS!

You've finished the Brain Quest Workbook!

All your hard work paid off! Ask a grown-up for help and cut out these SMART CARDS to make your own Brain Quest Mini-Deck.

You can play these anywhere—in the back of the car, at the park, or even at the grocery store. Remember: It's fun to be smart!®

Brain Quest Mini-Deck

QUESTIONS

MATH Order these numbers from least to greatest: <u>77</u>, <u>25</u>, <u>59</u>, <u>30</u>.

READING Which word doesn't belong here: <u>horse</u>, <u>cow</u>, <u>tree</u>, <u>pig</u>?

MATH What 3 numbers come right after 38?

READING "I like your green shoes." How many words are in this sentence?

BRAIN QUEST

QUESTIONS

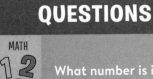
MATH What number is in the tens place in 146?

READING Say the words that begin with the same sound: <u>good</u>, <u>junk</u>, <u>gerbil</u>.

MATH Which month has more days: <u>January</u> or <u>February</u>?

READING "Milly drove the car to the store." Which word is the verb in this sentence?

BRAIN QUEST

QUESTIONS

MATH Janet plays soccer every Tuesday and Thursday. How many weekdays does she play?

LANGUAGE ARTS How do you spell the number 7?

MATH Which activity takes about 15 minutes: <u>eating breakfast</u> or <u>washing your hands</u>?

READING Which word means the same as *leave*: <u>depart</u> or <u>demand</u>?

BRAIN QUEST

QUESTIONS

MATH If 5 + 3 equals 8, what does 8 – 5 equal?

LANGUAGE ARTS Which letter do you NOT say in the word spelled w–r–i–s–t?

MATH Is 12 an <u>even number</u> or an <u>odd number</u>?

READING Take one word out of this command without changing its meaning: "You sit down."

BRAIN QUEST

QUESTIONS

LANGUAGE ARTS Which word has a long u sound: <u>mule</u>, <u>book</u>, <u>drum</u>?

READING Put this sentence in order: "the basket to me Give."

MATH The time on the clock is 1:00. What number does the minute hand point to?

LANGUAGE ARTS Put these parts of a story in the right order: <u>end</u>, <u>beginning</u>, <u>middle</u>.

BRAIN QUEST

QUESTIONS

MATH What is the sum of 14 plus 10?

LANGUAGE ARTS Which comes first in alphabetical order: <u>carrot</u>, <u>lettuce</u>, <u>broccoli</u>?

MATH What 5 coins add up to a nickel?

READING How do you change the word "toy" to make it mean more than one toy?

BRAIN QUEST

Brain Quest Grade 1 Workbook

Brain Quest Mini-Deck

ANSWERS

2 weekdays

MATH 1 2 3

s–e–v–e–n (seven)

LANGUAGE ARTS A B C

eating breakfast

MATH 1 2 3

depart

READING

BRAIN QUEST

ANSWERS

4
(1<u>4</u>6)

MATH 1 2 3

junk, gerbil

READING

January (It has 31 days; February has 28 days, or 29 in a leap year.)

MATH 1 2 3

"Milly <u>drove</u> the car to the store."

READING

BRAIN QUEST

ANSWERS

25, 30, 59, 77

MATH 1 2 3

tree (It's not an animal.)

READING

39, 40, 41

MATH 1 2 3

5 words

READING

BRAIN QUEST

ANSWERS

24
(14 + 10 = 24)

MATH 1 2 3

broccoli

LANGUAGE ARTS A B C

5 pennies
(1¢ + 1¢ + 1¢ + 1¢ + 1¢ = 5¢)

MATH 1 2 3

Add the letter s (toy<u>s</u>).

READING

BRAIN QUEST

ANSWERS

mule

LANGUAGE ARTS A B C

"Give the basket to me."

READING

the 12

MATH 1 2 3

beginning, middle, end

LANGUAGE ARTS A B C

BRAIN QUEST

ANSWERS

3

MATH 1 2 3

the letter w
(The letter w is silent in *wrist*.)

LANGUAGE ARTS A B C

an even number

MATH 1 2 3

"Sit down." (Take out the *you*.)

READING

BRAIN QUEST

Brain Quest Mini-Deck

QUESTIONS

 MATH — There are 2 dancers in 1 pair. How many dancers are in 3 pairs?

 READING — What three-letter word can you make from these letters: h–e–s?

 MATH — The table has 4 sides. Is it a <u>rectangle</u> or a <u>triangle</u>?

 MISCELLANY — What's the opposite of *hot*?

BRAIN QUEST

QUESTIONS

 MATH — In 15 minutes, it will be 2:45. What time is it now?

 **READING** — Which is a sentence? "A happy dream." or "Maria is dreaming."

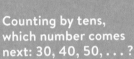 **MATH** — Counting by tens, which number comes next: 30, 40, 50, . . . ?

 READING — "i have seven french dolls." Which words in this sentence need a capital letter?

BRAIN QUEST

QUESTIONS

 MATH — Which does NOT add up to 9: <u>2 + 5</u>, <u>1 + 8</u>, <u>5 + 4</u>?

 MISCELLANY — "What time is it?" Is this a <u>question</u> or a <u>statement</u>?

 MATH — Each sandwich has 2 slices of cheese. Elsa ate 2 sandwiches. How many slices of cheese did she eat in all?

 READING — Which place comes first in alphabetical order: <u>school</u>, <u>home</u>, <u>bakery</u>?

BRAIN QUEST

QUESTIONS

 MATH — Mercedes took 7 apples and 6 oranges. Daniel took 6 apples and 4 oranges. Who took more fruit?

 READING — Which noun names a person: <u>classroom</u>, <u>teaching</u>, <u>teacher</u>?

 MATH — What is the sum of 12 + 13?

 READING — What's a longer way to say "I'm feeling tired"?

BRAIN QUEST

QUESTIONS

 MATH — What does the minus sign (–) tell you to do?

 LANGUAGE ARTS — Which word is spelled with one *e*: <u>bee</u> or <u>the</u>?

 MATH — It's 6:30. What time will it be in 1 hour?

 READING — What's the opposite of *tall*?

BRAIN QUEST

QUESTIONS

 MATH — Which is longer: <u>1 minute</u> or <u>1 hour</u>?

 READING — Which are rhyming words: <u>blue</u>, <u>do</u>, <u>show</u>?

 MATH — What 3 numbers come between 28 and 32?

 LANGUAGE ARTS — What is the fifth letter of the alphabet?

BRAIN QUEST

Brain Quest Mini-Deck

ANSWERS

MATH 1 2 3

2 + 5
(2 + 5 = 7)

MISCELLANY ?

a question

MATH 1 2 3

4 slices of cheese
(2 + 2 = 4)

READING

bakery

BRAIN QUEST®

ANSWERS

MATH 1 2 3

2:30

READING

"Maria is dreaming."
(A sentence tells a complete idea.)

MATH 1 2 3

60

READING

"I have seven French dolls."

BRAIN QUEST®

ANSWERS

MATH 1 2 3

6 dancers
(2 + 2 + 2 = 6)

READING

she

MATH 1 2 3

a rectangle

MISCELLANY ?

cold

BRAIN QUEST®

ANSWERS

MATH 1 2 3

1 hour (There are 60 minutes in 1 hour.)

READING

blue, do

MATH 1 2 3

29, 30, 31

LANGUAGE ARTS A B C

E

BRAIN QUEST®

ANSWERS

MATH 1 2 3

subtract

LANGUAGE ARTS A B C

the

MATH 1 2 3

7:30

READING

short

BRAIN QUEST®

ANSWERS

MATH 1 2 3

Mercedes (7 + 6 = 13 and 6 + 4 = 10; 13 is more than 10)

READING

teacher

MATH 1 2 3

25

READING

I am feeling tired.

BRAIN QUEST®

Brain Quest Mini-Deck

QUESTIONS

MATH
It is 8:00. What time will it be in 2 hours?

READING
What is the plural of the word *reptile*?

MATH
Every game had 3 innings. There were 2 games. How many innings were there in all?

MISCELLANY
How many colors are in a rainbow?

BRAIN QUEST

QUESTIONS

MATH
Which is longer: 9 inches or 6 inches?

LANGUAGE ARTS
What is the opposite of *late*: unhappy or early?

MATH
Which sign do you use to add numbers: + or − ?

READING
Is *curly* a noun or an adjective?

BRAIN QUEST

QUESTIONS

MATH
What are the next 3 numbers: 22, 23, 24, . . . ?

READING
Which noun names a place: friend, country, pickle?

MATH
Counting by tens, which numbers are missing: 60, ____, ____, 90?

LANGUAGE ARTS
Which word is the verb? "The cheetah ran across the savanna."

BRAIN QUEST

QUESTIONS

MATH
Is 83 an odd number or an even number?

LANGUAGE ARTS
Which comes first in alphabetical order: thunder, lightning, storm?

MATH
What is the name for a shape with 3 sides?

READING
Which is a sentence: "Bright morning sun." or "The sun sets in the west."?

BRAIN QUEST

QUESTIONS

MATH
Which does NOT equal 10: 3 + 7, 4 + 5, 2 + 8?

LANGUAGE ARTS
Which letter is silent in the word *castle*?

MATH
Find the sum of 17 and 8.

MISCELLANY
Is milk a solid or a liquid?

BRAIN QUEST

QUESTIONS

MATH
A pencil was 7 inches long. It was sharpened down 3 inches. How many inches is it now?

READING
Does the word *skunk* have a long u sound or a short u sound?

MATH
Which number is in the ones place in 186?

LANGUAGE ARTS
What is the next-to-last letter of the alphabet?

BRAIN QUEST

Brain Quest Mini-Deck

Card 1

ANSWERS

MATH 1 2 3

25, 26, 27

READING

country

MATH 1 2 3

60, <u>70</u>, <u>80</u>, 90

LANGUAGE ARTS A B C

"The cheetah <u>ran</u> across the savanna."

BRAIN QUEST®

Card 2

ANSWERS

MATH 1 2 3

9 inches

LANGUAGE ARTS A B C

early

MATH 1 2 3

+ (the plus sign)

READING

an adjective

BRAIN QUEST®

Card 3

ANSWERS

MATH 1 2 3

10:00

READING

reptiles

MATH 1 2 3

6 innings (3 + 3 = 6)

MISCELLANY ?

seven colors (red, orange, yellow, green, blue, indigo, and violet)

BRAIN QUEST®

Card 4

ANSWERS

MATH 1 2 3

4 inches (7 − 3 = 4)

READING

a short u sound

MATH 1 2 3

6
(18<u>6</u>)

LANGUAGE ARTS A B C

the letter y

BRAIN QUEST®

Card 5

ANSWERS

MATH 1 2 3

4 + 5
(4 + 5 = 9)

LANGUAGE ARTS A B C

the letter t (Cas<u>t</u>le)

MATH 1 2 3

25
(17 + 8 = 25)

MISCELLANY ?

a liquid

BRAIN QUEST®

Card 6

ANSWERS

MATH 1 2 3

an odd number

LANGUAGE ARTS A B C

lightning

MATH 1 2 3

a triangle

READING

"The sun sets in the west."

BRAIN QUEST®

Brain Quest Mini-Deck

QUESTIONS

 MATH Which two numbers are closest to 40: <u>35</u>, <u>42</u>, <u>51</u>?

 MISCELLANY "My hands are warm but my nose is cold." Which words mean the opposite?

 MATH If you have 3 shirts, 2 pairs of pants, and 1 dress, how many pieces of clothing do you have?

 MISCELLANY Which is NOT a month: <u>March</u>, <u>February</u>, <u>October</u>, <u>Thursday</u>?

BRAIN QUEST®

QUESTIONS

 **LANGUAGE ARTS** Which capital letter is made of three straight lines: <u>M</u>, <u>C</u>, <u>H</u>?

 MISCELLANY I say, "Woof." My name rhymes with *log*. What am I?

 MATH You have 3 groups of 5. What's your total?

 MISCELLANY What do you call a baby sheep?

BRAIN QUEST®

QUESTIONS

 MATH If 14 minus 7 equals 7, what does 15 minus 7 equal?

 LANGUAGE ARTS Which comes first in a dictionary: <u>wind</u> or <u>rain</u>?

 MATH How much is 6 + 6?

 READING Which words begin with the same sound: <u>photo</u>, <u>potato</u>, <u>final</u>?

BRAIN QUEST®

QUESTIONS

 MATH You have 4 pairs of socks. How many socks do you have?

 READING What's a shorter way to say "This playground does not have a slide."?

 MATH You have 1 bicycle and 2 unicycles. How many wheels do you have in all?

 READING What word can you add to *news* to name something you read?

BRAIN QUEST®

QUESTIONS

 MISCELLANY Which is smallest: a <u>flower</u>, a <u>bush</u>, or a <u>tree</u>?

 READING Which word is right for this sentence? "The monkeys (<u>is</u>/<u>are</u>) climbing."

 MISCELLANY How many days are in March?

 READING What's the word for more than one mouse?

BRAIN QUEST®

QUESTIONS

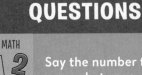 **MATH** Say the number that comes between 23 and 25.

LANGUAGE ARTS Which word spells a number: f-o-r-e or f-o-u-r?

MATH Julia went to the beach at 2 o'clock and stayed for 3 hours. What time did she leave?

LANGUAGE ARTS "Karl has three apples." Which words in this statement end with the same letter?

BRAIN QUEST®

Brain Quest Mini-Deck

ANSWERS

MATH 1 2 3
8
(15 − 7 = 8)

LANGUAGE ARTS A B C
rain

MATH 1 2 3
12

READING
photo, final

BRAIN QUEST

ANSWERS

LANGUAGE ARTS A B C
the letter *H*

MISCELLANY ?
a dog

MATH 1 2 3
15
(5 + 5 + 5 = 15)

MISCELLANY ?
a lamb

BRAIN QUEST

ANSWERS

MATH 1 2 3
35 and 42

MISCELLANY ?
"My hands are <u>warm</u> but my nose is <u>cold</u>."

MATH 1 2 3
6 pieces of clothing
(3 + 2 + 1 = 6)

MISCELLANY ?
Thursday (It is a day of the week.)

BRAIN QUEST

ANSWERS

MATH 1 2 3
24

LANGUAGE ARTS A B C
f–o–u–r (four or 4)

MATH 1 2 3
5 o'clock
(2 + 3 = 5)

LANGUAGE ARTS A B C
"Karl <u>has</u> three <u>apples</u>."

BRAIN QUEST

ANSWERS

MISCELLANY ?
a flower

READING
"The monkeys <u>are</u> climbing."

MISCELLANY ?
31 days

READING
mice

BRAIN QUEST

ANSWERS

MATH 1 2 3
8 socks
(2 + 2 + 2 + 2 = 8)

READING
"This playground <u>doesn't</u> have a slide."

MATH 1 2 3
4 wheels
(2 + 1 + 1 = 4)

READING
paper (newspaper)

BRAIN QUEST

YOU DID IT!

CONGRATULATIONS!

You completed every activity in the Brain Quest Grade 1 workbook. Write your name on the certificate below. Show your friends! Hang it on the wall! You should feel proud of your hard work.

CERTIFICATE OF
ACHIEVEMENT

Earned by

_____

for completing all sections in the
BRAIN QUEST®
GRADE 1 WORKBOOK